Java Interview Bootcamp

The practical guide to the Java interview process

Sam Atkinson

This book is for sale at http://leanpub.com/javainterviewbootcamp

This version was published on 2016-03-30

Leanpub

This is a Leanpub book. Leanpub empowers authors and publishers with the Lean Publishing process. Lean Publishing is the act of publishing an in-progress ebook using lightweight tools and many iterations to get reader feedback, pivot until you have the right book and build traction once you do.

To Laura. Thank you for (just about) putting up with me whilst I've been writing this and building the website. You're amazing.

To Mike & Dan for being an awesome support network and listening to me talk on and on and on about CJIQ all the time.

To Dave. Your incredible and tireless work as editor has made this a much better book than it would have been otherwise.

Contents

CONTENTS

Introduction

Welcome to Java Interview Bootcamp. Firstly, I'd just like to say a huge thank you to you for buying this book. I hope you will enjoy reading the book, but more importantly that it helps you to get your next amazing job.

Helping Java devs through the interview process is something I'm really passionate about. In my career I've interviewed hundreds of people from the most junior developers to the most senior technical leads. There have been some consistent themes throughout that really drove my desire to write this book and create www.corejavainterviewquestions.com. What I have learnt can be summed up in two key points; people are terrible at preparing for interviews, and they do not know how to give a good impression during an interview.

Programming interviews are both a skill and an art and as such they require practice and time. I have discovered most people simply don't take the time to prepare. A huge proportion of the developers I've interviewed struggle to answer basic java questions. They seem intentionally stand offish and make no effort to come across as personable. These are simple things that can be remediated with preparation. By purchasing this book you are already ahead of most of your competitors because you know that you need to take the time to study beforehand.

This book is split into two sections, interview process and core java revision. When someone is interviewing you they are looking to ensure that you are technically capable, but they also want to know that you are someone they can work with day to day. In the first half of the book we cover the different types of interview and what you can do as a candidate to make the best impression possible on your future employer.

The second half of the book is a ground-up revision of core java. The simple fact is in most interviews the technical questions bare little resemblance to our day-to-day programming. I've found most interview processes don't even involve a programming stage. Instead companies love to ask obscure threading questions or ask you to write java code on a whiteboard to reverse a string. Whether these are good interview questions or not isn't the subject of this book. The simple fact is you have to be prepared for them, which means spending some time to revise the basic core java principles.

I hope you find the everything you need in here. If you have any questions, queries, or just want to have a chat then you can email me on hello@corejavainterviewquestions.com. I will always respond.

If you're not already a member, don't forget to head to www.corejavainterviewquestions.com and sign up to the mailing list. It's packed with tons of valuable information and goodies.

Send me an email with your receipt for this book to hello@corejavainterviewquestions.com and I will send you back 2 example resumes and a practice interview too.

And last but not least: good luck with all your interviews. I'm sure you're going to knock them out the park.

Sam Atkinson, author of Java Interview Bootcamp.

Soft skills and process

Despite this being a Java focussed book, I honestly think the first half of this book is going to provide you with the most value. You're a Java developer. You have to have some idea what you're doing already (I hope). The second half of this book, focused on core Java and related questions, serves as a great way to revise and help relearn some areas that you've not touched in some time.

However, the simple fact is that for most candidates the struggle isn't with the technical side but with the softer skills. We ignore the importance of a handshake or a strong first impression at our peril. These are the areas that as geeks we suck at. We don't like talking to other people or giving presentations. Yes, these are generalisations but based on the candidates I've met they tend to ring true.

Work hard on this first section. Read it twice and make notes as you go through. Think about what stuff you didn't know that you need to start doing and think about where you're weak and need to improve, then go away and practice. Whether it be with a colleague or loved one, actually take the action to try things out before the interview. Do this and I guarantee you will stand yourself in the best stead for your hiring journey.

The interview process

Perhaps you're a fresh grad out of university and you've never looked for a job before and now you have absolutely no idea what you're doing. Alternatively it may just been a while since you last moved. In my experience developers fall into one of two categories: extremely fickle, moving jobs every 1-2 years, or insanely loyal and remaining with firms for well over 8 years. If you're in that latter group in particular then it can be daunting venturing out into the real world again.

The first sections of this book goes into great detail on each of the individual stages associated with the interview process, but first lets take a look at the process as a whole from a 50,000ft level.

Stage 1: Applying for jobs

The first step on the journey to better employment is simply getting your resume onto someones desk. How do you do this though?

Depending on your industry, the first port of call is probably to a recruiter. Recruiters act as the middle man between companies and potential hires, with the recruiting company getting paid based on them successfully placing a candidate into a role. Particularly in finance recruiters are the only option for getting your CV seen, as most firms don't have an easy way to directly submit your CV.

Recruiters have pros and cons. They have access to the entire market, they know what roles are available and it saves you having to manually search around for job roles. This saves a lot of time and effort. They handle the interaction with the new firm so you don't need to write cover letters or contact people directly. On the reverse though, not all recruiters are built equal. Some are brilliant and will only submit you for roles they think you'll excel at; they will guide you through the whole process and be understanding and work with you to get the right role. However, there are a lot out there who lack integrity and are laser focused on getting you into a job, whatever it is, so that they can get paid.

The best bet is to speak with friends and colleagues who have been through the process to see who they would recommend. I personally can highly recommend iKas (http://www.ikasinternational.com/) who have offices in London, New York, Australia, Singapore and Hong Kong, and BAH partners (http://www.bahpartners.com) who are exclusively Hong Kong.

If a recruiter is not an option then be prepared to work extra hard. You're going to have to manually hunt for roles and submit applications and covering letters. But how do you find the roles? There are a number of places online you can go to to find roles:

- http://careers.stackoverflow.com/
- Monthly "who's hiring" thread at HackerNews (https://news.ycombinator.com)

- LinkedIn. It's a gold mine. It has jobs directly advertised on the site, but you can also search for companies you like and follow them as they will advertise roles. Search for terms like "Java Jobs" in the groups section to find groups where companies directly advertise roles to.
- Job sites and job boards like jobaware.com, indeed.com, craigslist

This is not a fun process. You will be made to fill out your basic details over and over again, and you're likely going to need to write cover letters for each role. But this does mean you can very specifically tailor your search to particular firms, roles or areas.

Stage 2: Interviewing

Every firm has a different hiring process. Whilst one company may interview you face to face for an hour before making a decision another one may have you go through 7 stages of tests and interviews with different levels of seniority. If possible, ask what the process is from the earliest opportunity. Your recruiter or the hiring manager should be able to tell you. This should give you the most opportunity to prepare.

Below are the most common types of interview steps you can expect:

The phone interview

Phone interview's often come early on in the recruitment process. They're a great way to screen out candidates before bringing them in for a longer, more thorough interview. The interview will last anywhere between 15 minutes and an hour and will be focused on a limited subset of technical questions. Being on the phone limits the nature of the questions which can be asked as they all have to be verbal. Lack of whiteboard or pen and paper tends to make the interviews very theoretical or experience based, without much in the way of design.

Occasionally phone interviews can crop up later in the cycle, normally as a final round. This is normally after you've aced all of the other stages, and the manager who needs to sign off wants to have a chat with you. It should just be a formality, and normally involves questions about your experience and what you want from the role.

The at-home technical test

I'm a big fan of sending a homework to a candidate. It allows you to prove you are technically able without the pressure of being in an interview setting. Normally the exercise will take between one and three hours and will ask you to develop an effective solution to a problem, likely involving understanding of complex requirements, some sort of algorithm and maybe some threading. The important thing is to spend the time necessary to produce code that you are proud of before you submit. Any team that has this stage will value code quality highly so it's important not to cut corners.

The In-office technical test

There is a wider range of possibilities if you're asked to go in for a technical test. It could be a complete equivalent of the at home test; a number of firms don't trust candidates not to cheat at home (and from experience I know this does happen) and so ask them to do an exercise in the office. Normally it will be much shorter though and take a maximum of an hour.

As opposed to a single exercise, it's possible to receive a number of much smaller questions like an exam. This allows more focused questions on specific areas, and means that if you fail one section of it you can still pass the rest with flying colours.

My preferred method is the pair programming test. In this scenario you sit down with someone from the hiring team and program together through a predetermined exercise. Along with being tested on your technical ability the pairing exercise allows the hiring team to see how you work. Do you have a good grasp of keyboard shortcuts? Do you write tests first? Why did you choose to design this the way you did? If you get the job you will all be working together very closely, potentially for years to come. It's important not only that they like your coding style but that you like theirs.

Face to face

In person interviews are the best chance you have at landing a job, irrelevant of what stage in the process they are at. The simple fact is, people are biased. If you can sell yourself strongly to an interviewer then that person is going to be your biggest salesman. "I interviewed this guy and he was really good, we've got to bring him in". Often convincing a single person is all you need to grease the wheels of the entire interview process.

The face to face interview is likely to cover the broadest spectrum of questions and topics. Access to pens and paper or a whiteboard make this the best format to ask design questions in. Expect to be grilled about a system you've worked on before or asked to design something on demand. Similarly, interviewers love to ask people to write up pseudocode, particularly questions around creating search or sort algorithms. This tees the path up nicely for some big O type questions, but more importantly gives your potential employer the opportunity to see how you work through a problem.

One on one

The simplest interview. Person to person, normally for an hour or even more. This has the benefit that you are only trying to impress a single person, but this in turn means that if you get off on the wrong foot, or the person you're interviewing with is having a bad day then you have a problem. Try to get an understanding of who your interviewer is before you go to the interview if possible. From my experience these one to one meetings are normally with team leads or above, so whilst there will likely be some technical content the main purpose of the exchange is to understand how you are going to fit into the team and wider company culture.

Group grilling

Personally I think this is the most difficult of the interviews. Normally 2 or 3 of your potential new team members will be sat on the opposite side of the table throwing their best questions at you whilst you try your very best not to embarrass yourself. I find this interview the worst because impressing 3 people is really hard to do. Everyone has their own opinions and ways of working and the likelihood of you being able to satisfy all of your interrogators is slim.

Speed dating

The speed dating interview involves cramming in as many interviewers as possible within an allotted space of time. The default tends to be working through 3 separate interviewers. You remain in a room and interview with each one for 20 or 30 minutes, before they disappear and are replaced with yet more people asking different questions. I've even experienced this before when one of the interviewers has been dealing in using Video Conference. From an interviewers side this is great; you get a consensus opinion from a number of members of staff (anyone who gets a yes from all three is a definite pass) and it also means you can interview 3 candidates simultaneously. This is a really effective way of churning through people.

From the interviewee side however it can be intense. That's a lot of interviewing! If you're just doing 1 hour with one or two people then once you're in the flow things are good. You can get comfortable with your interviewer. However seeing lots of different interviewers means you can't relax. You're constantly trying to figure out what each person is looking for. It is really hard work, and there is no way to prepare for it beyond regular java preparation. The best advice I can give you if going in for one of these is to remember that everyone's different. Although generally there will be team themes (maybe they all love Test Driven Development) the individuals will all like different facets, prefer different technologies. As with any interview, try to strike up a rapport with the person on the other side of the table. Whilst obviously it is important to be technically able, a huge percentage of you success is going to come down to whether the interviewer likes you and your attitude.

Example interview process

To give you an idea of what to expect, here are some example processes I've gone through before:

- **Major Australian Bank**:
    - One on One Interview with team manager
    - Aptitude test
    - 2 hour technical interview; 1 hour face to face with local developer, 1 hour with 2 developers over Video Conference
    - Interview With Department Heads
- **Small Charity Firm**
    - Face to Face with future manager and department head

- – HR Interview
- **Major International Bank**
  - – 30 Minute phone interview
  - – Pair Programming interview with 2 developers
  - – Group Grilling with 3 developers

Creating your resume

You only get one opportunity for a first impression, From which point it's either working for you or against you. This applies across all media, from websites (where you have 7 seconds to impress the visitor) to meeting a new person at an interview (where you have even less). Getting off on the wrong foot means you need to be incredibly impressive to stand a chance of landing your new role, which whilst not impossible is certainly going to make a difficult interview even harder. On the other hand if you arrive and can make a bond with an interviewer then the job is yours to lose; psychologically they're going to be rooting for you to do well, so as long as you don't make any major mistakes then the person on the other side is going to do try his best to get you hired.

"But how does this relate to my CV?" I hear you cry. Your CV is your very first first impression. When the interviewer reads your resume it is the first time they have been exposed to you and what you stand for. Interviewers receive hundreds of CVS for every role so understandably very few of them stand out as exciting. Let's be clear; your CV is a sales document. After reading your hard crafted words you want whoever is reading it to turn to the person next to them and say â€œhey, this guy looks really good. We should bring him in soon". I would say this happens for me every 20 CVs or so.

Before we dive into crafting the perfect programmer's propaganda, I have one crucial piece of advice that applies not just to CVs but to all of the hiring and interview processes that you're going to go through.

Killer advice: Everyone is different

All of the people you are going to talk to during the interview process will have differing opinions on what makes a good developer. If there was a standardised exam or some other way of telling a good developer from a bad one then it would make hiring a whole lot easier (and no, being a Sun Certified Java Programmer does not even come close). Every interview you go to is going to have different questions and each interviewer is going to have a different set of values. One may value polyglot developers. Another may value TDD and BDD. The next may believe all code should be done in notepad and hand compiled. There is no golden bullet.

As a candidate it can be hard to remember this. Perhaps your CV isn't getting you interviews, or maybe you've been on a couple of interviews and haven't progressed. Your head drops and you conclude that you're stuck where you are and that you're not good enough to get a new job.

The reality is that you've just not found a place that aligns with your values yet, and that's ok.

What you want from a job may make it easier or harder for you to find a role. For me, I hate big-o notation and performance questions because I have google nearby and I believe people have a tendency to prematurely optimise code; real performance problems happen very rarely. That means there are interviews where I come out and I know I have done terribly, *and I don't care.* I'm comfortable knowing I don't want to work for that team because their values don't align with mine. Does that make it harder for me to get a job? Yes, but it means that when I find a role it's the one that I really want. You spend most of your waking life at work, so you may as well spend the time to get it right.

This is a roundabout way of saying that there is no golden template for your resume. You can send a CV to 5 different people and get 5 different responses. All you can do is bullet proof your document so you don't have stupid things like spelling errors (which happens a lot) and then use your text to craft a message that makes you as desirable as possible to the type of people you want to work for.

Resume format

How long should it be?

This is the source of much debate. My view is vehemently that if possible, it should be one page (with an absolute maximum of two). People don't have time to read resumes in detail and they don't care what school you went to or your last 15 jobs. They want a brief sales pitch about why your skills fit the job. By keeping it brief and packed with only important information you're making the job much easier for the reader whilst demonstrating your ability to communicate concisely.

On the other side it should be noted that in the past I have been told by recruiters to bulk out my CV. If you're working with a recruiter they will often cut up and edit your CV as appropriate for roles anyway. As a result I keep 2 copies of my CV; the first is a brief, single pager with my key roles and experience condensed down. The other is a 2 pager with as much stuff crammed in as possible for recruiters to work with.

Do not be tempted to create a 15 page tome with thousands of words. When I receive these it's an instant red flag. Bigger is not better and you're just highlighting your inability to communicate effectively. If the company needs your history going back 15 years then they will come and ask you for it at a later date. A resume is your sales document to say what your best skills are with clear examples of you using those skills to achieve great things. Let me say that again. **Your CV is your opportunity to say what your best skills are**. It should be achievement focused, showing what your amazing talents are, and what they've helped you to achieve.

Opening blurb

Not all candidates include this but I think it's the most important part. This is a single paragraph introduction to you and your brand. What do you stand for? What do you care about? Think of this as your elevator pitch, where you can outline what makes you great and why someone should hire you. Talk about what your passions are; maybe you love TDD, or you think of yourself as the tsar of concurrency. Start off with this. It's a nice way to set the stall at the start of the document.

Avoid being tacky in your opening blurb. Don't forget there is a person on the other side that's going to be reviewing this; candidates seem to love piling in as many buzzwords as they can: "self motivating with attention to detail". What does that even really mean? I can guarantee the person reading your CV won't know. If someone asked you during the interview what about you exemplifies those skills could you answer it? I'm guessing not convincingly. Aim to write in a clean and simple fashion. If there are some buzzwords you want to put make sure that you have the material to back it up; my CV talks about how I'm a passionate technologist, which I then back up with outside of work projects and examples of where I've used that passion in my roles.

The simple fact is, most of it won't get read. The person recruiting has a lot of these to read through so will likely read only this paragraph and if you're lucky skim the rest. Get this section right and put your most impressive material first.

Employment history

You don't need more than the last 5 years or the last 3 roles, whichever is smaller. This should be brief and focus on what **you** produced and how **you** did it. It's incredible how many summaries I read which tell me all about the history of company X where the candidate worked and the ambitious project that company was executing. That tells me nothing about the person behind the resume. Here is an example of what not to do:

"Senior Java Developer, Awesome Co. July 2012- July 2014

Awesome Co. are one of the worlds leading investment banks. Based in New York and with offices around the world the company prides itself on a customer centric approach to banking.

I was working on Project X. This project was a 200m investment to create a next generation banking platform over an ambitious 3 year period based on Java and NoSQL technology. The project has a strong focus on agile delivery and creating a low latency system"

You'll notice there's almost no reference to the candidate. Too many programmer resumes are formed like this. Compare this instead to the following resume example:

"Senior Java Developer, Awesome Co. July 2012- July 2014

Successfully lead a team of 6 developers using agile methodologies and iterative delivery on an ambitious timeline to produce an industry leading platform.

- I introduced the use of iterative delivery and story planning which allowed us to accurately predict our velocity and allowed us to consistently deliver to production every 2 weeks.

- I created a comprehensive NFT framework which allowed us to run regressions quickly and ensure we were meeting the high standards set by the business

- Led the design of the system and introduced ActiveMQ and MongoDB to produce an exceptionally quick and easily tested system; all code was built using TDD"

This time the entire article is focused on the candidate. I now know what they have done and what they have achieved. It's a much more convincing sales pitch.

Also, people love lists. A list of achievements is much easier to parse. Use lists as much as possible!

Extra curricular activities

If you've done stuff in your job which is extra to your regular role you need to shout about it. The best candidates want more than to come in, code for 8 hours and then go home. If you've been on a course or training that you think is pertinent then put it down. Here's some ideas; if you've not got any of these then start doing them now!

- Any innovation projects you may have done, or tools and techniques pioneered. For example, maybe you introduced JIRA into your organisation.
- Organised guest speakers to come and speak to the team.
- Organised teams to do presentations to each other in a weekly forum.
- Contributions to Open Source.
- Member of a community such as an agile group.
- Participated in events like Startup Weekend or Angelhack.

It's this kind of extra work that can make you a stand out candidate in a competitive marketplace.

Education

99% of people reading your CV will not care about your education. A lot of programmers have come from non CompSci backgrounds, and some don't even have degrees. Your vocational experience is infinitely more important in a development role. Include your degrees, and maybe a line on your A Levels, nothing more. Put this section at the end of the document. It's unimportant so waste as little space as possible on it.

List of technologies

Don't do it. For some reason more and more resumes come with a list of every technology the candidate has ever touched. Some CVs even have scores on them now to say how proficient in each technology the applicant is. If you know a role is keen for a specific technology then tailor your experience section to explain how you're awesome at this. If you have stuff you want to cover off that hasn't been suitable in any other section then have a small "skills" section. Whatever you do, don't just write a list of technologies. It impresses no one and the interviewer could call you out on any of those technologies. If you don't feel comfortable being able to answer in depth interview questions on a technology then don't list it!

There are some great tips related to this and building a good CV in the Core Java Interview Questions Podcast with Sarah Sellers, a recruiter with a lot of experience in helping candidates out. You can listen at http://www.corejavainterviewquestions.com/podcast5.

Top tips for standing out as a candidate

- If you've done any "extras" in previous roles, then put these in. It proves that you go "above and beyond" in your role.
- If you have personal projects or shared projects you contribute to then list these. Candidates with their github on the CV make a big impression as it shows you like coding so much you go home and do even more of it. That's passion.
- If you have a personal website or blog then include it, but make sure it looks good and has been updated in the last 6 months. I've seen some terrible candidate websites, and it instantly puts me off. Make sure your site is looking good and up to date and it can absolutely earn you some extra credit.
- If you've been playing around with technologies at home then list them and what you've been doing with them. A lot of organisations will limit the permitted technologies you are allowed to use; if you then go home and play with NoSQL or node.js then by putting this on your resume you are displaying a wider awareness of technology which is a sought after skill.

Make it look pretty

I'm being very serious when I say most CVs don't stand out. They're just blocks of text going into pages and pages. Having just a little bit of design can make a big difference. I'm a huge fan of google docs for this; they have some basic attractive templates which can make you stand out just a little from the rest of the pile. It's not much, but it's often enough.

Phone interviews

I'm a huge fan of using a phone interview at the start of my hiring process. As someone trying to recruit it's important that I have some way of filtering the hundreds of candidates that get sent through. I've come to accept most people are terrible at writing a resume, and some just plain bend the truth, so before I meet someone face to face I find it's useful to speak to them on the phone for 20 minutes to ensure that they do know java and get an understanding of their background. As a candidate it's also an opportunity to make a good first impression. Many people panic that they won't be able to do themselves justice over the phone (and indeed, candidates who fail often cite this as a reason); however with a few pieces of key advice you can be sure to come out on top of the pack.

Preparing for your Java phone interview

You may be dealing with a recruiter or with the firm directly. Either way, contact them and find out the exact details of the phone interview. You want to be as prepared as you can be. Specifically you should ask:

- How long will it be?
- What sort of questions will be asked? You'll be lucky if you get an answer to this, but it's good to know if the questions are more likely to be technical focused or design focused. Phone interviews tend to have a technical slant as design interviews are really hard to do without a piece of paper or a whiteboard. It's certainly worth asking as you might hit lucky and get some gems of information to help you in your preparations.
- How many people will be on the call? Who will they be? Phone interviews with one or two people will generally be easier as you can identify who's who and an understanding of their interests and question style. Above that will make it a little more difficult.

It's then time to simply to hit the books and get revising. Chances are you're going to get a lot of "what does this thing in Java do?" type questions, as they're easy to do over the phone. They're not necessarily good questions, but they're the questions interviewers tend to fall back on.

Make sure that whenever you've booked your interview for you have **somewhere quiet and private to go**. Make sure you get there **5 minutes** before the interviewer is due to call. There is nothing worse than starting your call flustered because you don't have a place to do the interview and it leaves a terrible first impression. As an interviewer I have a limited amount of time; I tend to bunch phone interviews to be back to back or slip them in between meetings. If you waste 5 minutes then you're losing an opportunity to impress the interviewer.

Make sure you **have a copy of your CV with you**. The interviewer will have a copy too and will ask you about it. I would guess that you can't remember what you've written on your resume so have it in front of you. It's very embarrassing when someone asks you about a part of your CV and you have no idea what they're talking about.

Ensure you go in with a **pre-prepared list of questions for the end of the interview**. You will get asked and it's important that you are quick to respond. I want to know that you care about the role I'm hiring for and have spent 30 seconds to look at the job description and that want to know more. Interviewers (and people in general) are egotistical. It doesn't matter if it's a simple "I was hoping you could tell me more about the role"; just make sure you don't spend 5 seconds in silence as if you hadn't expected the question to be asked. Have 2 or 3 questions lined up. It doesn't matter if you really want an answer, the act of asking is what matters.

For the exceptionally lazy, here's a list of example questions:

- Please can you tell me a bit more about the team? What size is it? What experience levels?
- Is the team based in one region or geographically split?
- How does the team work? Do you use agile?
- What's your biggest frustration in your current job?
- What's your favourite part of working at the company and in the team?
- What does an average day look like?
- How hard is it to use new technologies in your company?
- What training exists?

It's also an opportunity to impress and show off. Say you know the people who are interviewing you are really keen on a technology or technique, like Test Driven Development. Use your questions to promote yourself! "I'm a huge fan of TDD and was wondering how exactly do you use it in your team?". Or "I've always wanted to learn TDD but have never been given the opportunity. I find the concept really exciting. Do you think the learning curve is manageable?". This is music to an interviewers ears because you actually care. If I'm doing 3 interviews a day, 5 days a week things like this really make a big difference.

Tips for giving the best impression

When your phone rings, think positive. Be positive. Sound happy. As cheesy as this sounds, the old adage of "you have 7 seconds to make a first impression" is spot on. The amount of candidates I call that sound grumpy and/or uninterested is crazy. This instantly turns an interviewer against you and unless you nail all the questions you're going to have a hard time getting through. Conversely, if you pick up the phone, sound excited and tell the interviewer you've been looking forward to the interview then you're in the positive books from the start.

Speak slowly. You don't want to rattle through the interview at lightning pace but don't speak so slowly as to bore the interviewer. Most importantly, know when to stop. I've had candidates give me 5 minute monologues on Spring before I've had to step in. Being able to craft a succinct answer is a hugely important skill, not just in interviewing but as a java developer. It takes practice but it is well worth it. If you're worried about not answering the question fully, simply say "is that ok or would you like me to continue?". Chances are the interviewer will have picked up on something you've mentioned and will change the direction of the question or ask a new one. If not they may simply ask you to continue and you can keep talking. Some quick don'ts:

- Don't sound bored
- Don't chew gum
- Don't google answers (**we can hear the keyboard**)
- Don't interrupt the interviewer
- Don't be afraid to say you don't know. Trying to guess your way through isn't going to fool anyone. If I'm asking the question then I probably know the answer. It's absolutely fine to say "I don't know about that, but I'm happy to try and work it out if you'd like". That way everyone knows you're not trying to lie your way through. Candidates capable of admitting they don't know will always gain respect.

What you will get asked during the interview

Due the limitations of the telephone you can be fairly certain that the questions will be based in one of four categories:

- Core Java: threading, exceptions, data structures & algorithms, object oriented programming etc. This is the basic stuff you simply need to take the time to revisit. Whether or not they are good questions to ask to determine your ability is irrelevant; most interviews will fall back on this so it's good to be prepared. Reading the second half of Java Interview Bootcamp is the best place to start.
- Technology discussion. "Have you used technology X (or "I see from your CV you've used X)?", "Can you tell me about it? What do you think of it?". My default go-to topics are Spring and Hibernate as they have a lot of questions that can lead from the initial one and really go into depth. They also appear on most people's CVs. This is the sort of question I prefer to ask as you can get a proper understanding of a candidate's knowledge and whether they understand the tools they use, or if they just use them because they're told. Look at the core technologies on your resume and figure out what your opinion is on them. The interviewer most likely won't care what the opinion is specifically, more that you can articulate the pros and cons of each side and draw a conclusion.
- Techniques. I love asking about these. Every office works differently; agile vs waterfall (yes, waterfall still exists), TDD/BDD/other DD, programming style etc. Again, if you have put these on your CV then you need to be sure you have good answers for **your** experience with them. If your department uses TDD so you've put it on the CV but you don't actually do it you're going to look bad. Again review your CV and look at what you've listed; come up with strong explanations for each of them.

- Riddles. This is made up of the google-esque questions like "how many grains of sand are there in the world?" and "What would you do if you were stuck in a lift for an hour and a half?". It's good to try and read up on some of these just to get comfortable with answering them, but in reality they're not something you can do a great amount of study for. Personally I'm not a big fan of these, but every interviewer is different.

Try not to guess what the interviewer is looking for or what you think the interviewer believes is the "right" answer. They may intentionally lead you down the wrong path to see if you're a "yes man". Stick to your opinions even if they seem controversial. Be polite, be honest, and try to engage in an open discussion. The person on the other side of the phone isn't a robot so try and engage the human side and have a 2 way conversation. If a candidate fires a question back at me during an answer I tend to enjoy it. An interview should be two way.

After the interview

Normally you should have a pretty good idea of how you've done, but don't fret. I've had candidates who thought they'd tanked who were actually really good. Conversely I've had terrible people who thought they had done brilliantly. Simply wait to hear back from them and relax comfortable in the knowledge you've done your best. If you don't make it through then don't sweat it. The fact is that every interviewer is different and has different opinions, every company values different things and you may not fit into the team at that time. That's ok. Just keep applying to different roles.

On top of this there is a human element; maybe the interviewer woke up on the wrong side of the bed, or they haven't had lunch yet so they're hungry. It's terrible to think that this could affect your potential job but it's a fact of life. Whatever you do, don't contest the result. Emailing back to try and explain something better now you've had time to think about it or asking to be seen again isn't going to work and may damage your reputation. The industry is surprisingly small (particularly thanks to LinkedIn) so hold your head high, take the time to review what you could have done better for next time and move on.

Face to face interview

The vast majority of interviews you are likely to undertake during a recruitment process will be a variation of the face to face interview: as discussed earlier in the book, there are a huge number of variations a recruiter can pick and choose from. Although there are tips and tricks specific to each one there are some key tenets that run through them all which enable you to best represent yourself as a candidate. Whilst having the technical skills for the role is obviously crucial the reality is that success is often determined by gut feel- whether or not the interviewers have a good "feeling" about you. You can influence by the way you present yourself; your handshake, the conversations you have and your body language. In my experience these things end up being massively influential when making a decision about a candidate.

First impressions

It is cliche, and I've already said it multiple times, but first impressions really are everything. The initial meeting can be the difference between success and failure even though you've not answered a single question. Although I think any bias is unconscious, people will ask easier questions of candidates that they like from the initial introduction alone (and vice versa harder questions for difficult candidates.)

But what makes a good first impression?

Turning up on time: It's baffling that this needs to be written down but the number of candidates I've had arrive late is incredible. You are being interviewed by busy people who are taking the time out of their day to sit with you. The moment you arrive late you're in the "no" column and fighting to escape. Ideally try to arrive about 5 minutes before the scheduled start time. It is also important not to arrive too early. I know everywhere I've ever worked has struggled for meeting room space and if you get there really early it puts the burden onto the interviewer to find somewhere for you to wait. You don't want to have them pulled out of an important meeting to deal with your arrival because you've turned up far too soon.

Dressing Correctly: It varies by industry, but I've found generally people don't bother with a full suit and tie combination anymore, generally just wearing trousers and a shirt. I think this is preferable and will help you to relax. If you feel more comfortable wearing a suit then go for it, you're not going to get marks against for dressing too formally (although I would recommend taking your suit jacket off when you get to the interview itself). However, make sure that whatever you wear fits properly: don't be the classic stereotype of a geek wearing a suit two sizes too large.

I've had people show up to interviews in jeans and a t-shirt before. Don't do that ever. You will never make a bad impression by dressing up too much, however you certainly will by dressing too casually.

Handshake: Never underestimate the importance of a good handshake. There are three types of handshake. The first is the weak, limp shake which a lot of geeks suffer from as we tend to be timid. You are making a statement about the type of person you are with your handshake. If yours has no-pressure then the conclusion is you are weak in the office: less likely to stand up at the whiteboard or to have strong opinions. All from just a handshake!

The second sort of handshake is the bone crusher. At the very other end of the spectrum is the type of person who has heard that a strong handshake is important and as a result attempts to crush the other persons hand as a show of force and strength. Again, avoid this. It signifies you are an overbearing personality or you're overcompensating for something. It also hurts! This is equally as bad as the limp handshake.

Instead we want the third shake, the Goldilocks of handshaking: just right. A good handshake conveys confidence but without being over the top. It is firm, with good pressure, but without leaving the other person feeling they need to go to hospital with a broken hand. Unsurprisingly this takes practice. So practice! Ask your close colleagues, friends or family to practice with you. It can take only 3 minutes of testing out different pressures to figure out what a good handshake is for you but it can make a huge difference in your first impression. I was lucky enough in school to have a teacher who ran a lesson dedicated to this and it has stood me in good standing ever since.

First conversation: The awkward moment where you finally have to talk. The two major things you need to consider here are what you want to say, and how you're going to say it.

Body language, mannerisms and tone are all understandably important. Your job is to convey to the interviewer that you are excited for the interview and job opportunity. You would be surprised by the number of candidates who sound like they have no interest in being at the interview. If your tone is dull and you sound like this is just another interview your recruiter is putting you through then why should the interviewer be willing to spend his time with you? Sound interested. Sound excited. Sound like you want the job!

Go into your interview with some ideas for small talk. Again, we programmers tend to be a quiet bunch lacking in conversational skills. Chances are there's going to be some point from when you're collected in reception to the interview starting where you're going to need to fill the gap with conversation. This is a great opportunity for you to sell yourself, whether you're talking about something you're working on at the moment or just being honest about your nerves. It's a chance to make a good impression and to bond with your interviewer. If you're really struggling then ask questions. "What are you working on at the moment?". "I was reading up on Java 8 last night, have you seen the new stuff on default methods?". It allows the other person to talk and takes the pressure off you, and is also a great way to build a relationship. People are usually better at talking than listening and will be pleased you're asking questions and giving them the chance to talk. It sounds cheesy but it's true.

Interview formats

Once you've made your incredible first impression, the hard work begins. Depending on the stage of the interview the content may vary greatly so it's important to know what you're going in for. Make sure you talk to your recruiter or the hiring company beforehand and ask what will be involved in the interview; how many people, how many stages, what sort of questions. Normally companies are happy to release this information to help you prepare. Never forget that the people interviewing you want you to get the job. They want you to be the amazing developer they've been looking for and you need to prove to them it's you.

Technical interview

This is the bread and butter of most interview processes, and the main focus of this book. A group of developers asking you a series of questions on java programming, algorithms and design. This is always going to be the most difficult part of any interview process. The domain space is so huge you could get asked anything, and some interviewers pride themselves on asking esoteric questions. However, most people aren't like that and will limit themselves to a core set of questions.

In preparation for a Java interview you have to make sure you've revised the core material. Even though you spend all day every day working in the code the fact is that most of the "complicated" parts of the language are infrequently used but regularly asked in interviews. At a minimum you need to revise the big three:

- Threading
- Collections
- Garbage Collection

A natural extension on collections is to study algorithms as the questions will often revolve around writing an algorithm to sort a data structure. These too are covered later in the book.

You are also quite likely to be asked about your design experience. One that seems to pop up regularly is "tell me about something you've designed" or "tell me about the system you're working on at the moment". Normally you will be given a whiteboard and asked to sketch out the architecture and asked to explain as you go along. This is a nice open ended question and can give you a good opportunity to show off by engaging in discussions around technology choices and resilient design.

Finally you are likely to get asked "fluffy" questions. A huge amount of being a developer has absolutely nothing to do with code. Development practices is a great example; I love to ask candidates about their experience with agile development for example. It allows a clear delineation between people who just do what they're told and people who take an active interest in the development practices and understand their purposes. There's also the non-technical questions that fit into this section: "What excites you about going to work?" is another one of my favourites.

When answering these loose open ended questions don't feel the need to launch straight into an answer and blab your way through. It's ok to take the time up front to think of a good answer. This is not the sort of information people keep ready in their heads and the interviewer knows that.

The Management Interview

After you've cleared the hurdles of the developer team you will normally end up in a room with a manager. This may be the team manager (who will likely still be technical to some degree) or it may be a department head (who is quite removed from the day to day). The likelihood is that this is going to focus heavily on the interpersonal fluffy questions. The purpose of this interview is to get an understanding of your experience as part of a team, to figure out your potential as an employee and to determine if you will be a good fit for the team and the company.

There is no right answer to these questions and it will depend entirely on the values of the person interviewing you and the firm you're interviewing with. Some firms are looking for people who can bring a breath of fresh air and stir things up, people to bring new ideas and mix things up. Once when I was being interviewed by a head of development I spent a huge amount of time talking about the importance of continuous delivery and having to build monitors as information radiators, all of which he had heard about but had never tried to implement. By showing I could bring some valuable new skills to the team he was exceptionally keen to hire me.

Conversely, a large proportion of the people who interview you will be looking for people who can slot in seamlessly with the team or company and hit the ground running. If you know someone who's already working there you can find out what "good" looks like to that team/company and tailor your answers accordingly, but most of the time you won't know what your interviewer is specifically looking for. Don't worry about this, and don't try and guess based on the intonation or questions asked. Just be honest and try to show where your expertise and passion lies. The simple reality is not everyone will fit in everywhere, and that's ok. Just talk candidly about your experiences and opinions and try and strike up interesting conversations.

Be confident and outgoing. Even though the person you're talking to is in management it's no reason to get nervous. Think of the worst case scenario: you don't get the job. That's ok. Most of your peers will struggle with this interview as it's heavily focused on being able to give articulate answers and have interactive conversations. If this is not your strong point then *practice*. Ask a friend (preferably not in IT) to drill you on these questions until you no longer sound nervous.

Example Questions

- What do you enjoy about going to work?
- What do you dislike about being a developer?
- Why are you leaving your current job?
- If you could change one thing about your current team what would it be?
- What does a good team look like?
- What makes a good developer?

- Tell me about a time you had conflict at work. How did you deal with it?
- Tell me about the biggest mistake you made at work?

Technical tests

What are technical tests?

Over the years I've tried many different types of ways of screening candidates; phone interview, speed dating style, full on technical interview and everything in between. My favourite method by far is the technical test, also known as the coding homework.

The technical test is simply an exercise or set of exercises given for you to complete at home. Normally it will take one to two hours and will be reasonably challenging, involving some level of complexity such as Threading or algorithms. The instructions will likely be emailed to you, giving you a certain time frame within which to complete it.

Why are they good?

Most interview process do not involve the candidate writing any code. This is crazy! You're interviewing to be a programmer and most job interviews don't involve you doing any programming. If you're lucky enough to be in a process which does involve looking at your code there are 3 main options they could use:

- Bring you in and watch you code. This could be a pair programming exercise or it could be simply sitting you in front of an exercise and watching you code. I'm a big fan of the pair programming interview as a mechanism to use later on in the interview cycle to get a good understanding of how a programmer interacts with other people and designs their way through a solution.
- Ask for a code sample. Less popular than it used to be, but the equivalent of asking a graphic designer for their portfolio. Most the code people write is for their employer and cannot be exported outside the firm, so it relies on the hiree having personal projects to showcase. I'd recommend if you do already have projects that you upload them to github and include them on your CV: you look good for having the project and it shows you're proud of your code.
- The Technical Test!

The problem with a pairing interview is that it takes a lot of time out of the hirer's day, often 2 people taking 2 hours per candidate. This is expensive, and so it is better saved to the end of the process. Code samples on the other hand aren't standardised. They give a view on what your code style is, but are unlikely to answer all of the questions the interviewer has about your ability. It also means as an interviewer I need to get myself around a new problem space and code base for each and every candidate which takes a lot of time and effort.

Coding Homeworks on the other hand take relatively little time to review. They're standardised, which makes the recruiting team's job easier and ensures candidates are compared on a level playing field. The challenge can be written to ensure it tests whatever facets the company values; algorithms, threading, design etc. Personally I find them a great first or second stage interview to sort the wheat from the chaff and immediately filter out a huge number of candidates. A lot of people talk big game on their CV but are terrible programmers.

However be wary of using this too early in the process if you're putting a hiring process together. I've had a number of candidate's refuse to do the interview when they've not even had a phone interview yet. When asking a candidate to take 1 or 2 hours out to write code they will often want the opportunity to talk to you first so they can get more information on the role and make sure it's worth their time. On the other hand I've also had candidates who are extra excited for the role because it's shown we value a candidates ability to code highly, a very desirable attribute.

How to pass

This may sound obvious, but a the very minimum you need to produce something that compiles, runs and solves the problem. I've reviewed far too many submissions where the code simply didn't compile. This is a straight no. Don't expect the reviewer to spend a lot of time trying to get things working. Use a standard build tool like maven and include clear, step by step instructions in a readme file.

Ensure you read and follow the instructions to the letter. I once had someone submit a solution in Scala despite the instructions specifying Java. This just wastes everyone's time. If you are at all unsure then ask. Chances are you won't be the first person to have the issue, and if you are then they can amend their instructions for future candidates.

Your target should be to write code you would be happy to see go into production. At the highest level, I'm looking to see if the very best code you can produce (which is what this should be) is good enough that I'd be happy for you to commit to my codebase. Clearly "good code" is a very personal opinion but if you submit something you're proud of then that is the best you can do. If you don't pass because of the code style you can rest assured that the team is not a good fit for you. As an example; If I was rejected from a team because I didn't comment my code I'd be glad I missed out because I believe that code should be written with good naming and broken down so that it's clear what's going on without comments (with the exception of APIs). Your code is a representation of what you value.

Some key things to check before you submit: - All methods, classes, tests and variables are consistently named - Remove all commented out code - Don't leave unused code in; a good IDE like IntelliJ[1] will clearly highlight if a piece of code isn't being referenced - Delete any unused classes or tests - Remove any main methods you wrote "just to test if something worked" - Remove all breakpoints! They show up if the reviewer uses the same IDE

---

[1]http://cjiq.co/intellij

Above and beyond this it simply comes down to creating a good solution that solves the problem. Read the question thoroughly and jot down what the concerns are. Is the problem latency sensitive? Is there a large data volume? If a UI is involved is there a responsiveness concern? If you write a list of what's important (and what's not) it will give you a good guide when creating your solution so you can optomise the right things. Do not prematurely optomise! If the solution asks you to read in a file of 10 lines, don't write an incredible caching solution. It's 10 lines!

Make sure to write tests. Tests are great anyway, but if you have tests written for the key requirements you can be sure that you've ticked them off whilst proving to the creator you've read, understood and coded for them.

Once you've finished, put your solution into whatever format requested (zip, github, jar) along with your comprehensive readme and email it to another computer. If you have a spare laptop then great, if not then maybe a friend's. Try it out on here before you submit it; you want to ensure you avoid the issue of "Works On My Machine" where it looks fine on your laptop but works nowhere else because of some esoteric setting or an assumption you've made. If you can send it to someone and they can get it up and running with no guidance then you're good to go. Send it in and keep your fingers crossed!

Following the technical test

What comes next depends entirely on who is hiring you. Some people will give you a simple pass/fail with no feedback. In this scenario go back and ask for feedback anyway. If you've failed then it can be comforting to know why so you can improve next time (or perhaps it was a style issue as mentioned, in which case you can rest in peace). Even if you've passed it can be good to know any areas the team felt you could have improved on. This way you can allay these fears in the next round.

A common practice is to bring you in to discuss the code. I really like this as a concept. Often code cannot explain a design decision by itself and it can be a good platform for the hirer to understand how you think. Why did you model the domain like you did? Why did you use composition over inheritance? Before the interview spend an hour looking over your code trying to think of questions and preparing answers. Saying "I don't know" about why you crafted your code in a certain way does not look good. Design and implementation decisions should be deliberate. Some key questions I like to ask of candidates:

- Why did/didn't you make this final? Is this immutable?
- Are there any threading issues here?
- This code seems quite complicated. Why did you write it this way? Is there any way you could simplify it?
- You've written comments here. Why?
- Why did you choose ArrayList/LinkedList/Other thing?
- Are there any third party libraries that could've helped you with this?
- You've overridden equals/hashcode. Why? What changed as a result?

- For anything where speed is a concern. Did you test this to see if it made a difference?

Remember, there is rarely a "right" answer. The questions are there to prompt a discussion and to see if you understand the concerns of each choice. Don't feel the need to make stuff up or compromise because you think the interviewer is looking for a certain answer. Stick to your opinions and have a sensible discussion!

Tell me about your system

This is one of my absolute upmost favourite questions to ask during a face to face interview. Right now in your current role you'll be working on a system (maybe more than one), and you've put hours of your life into it. You probably have a bunch of guys and girls you've worked with to put the system live and deliver some awesome value to someone. This should be the one thing that you know really really well. Nonetheless the number of candidates that get caught out by this question is incredible. You wouldn't believe how much some people struggle with this.

Why are you getting asked this question?

For the interviewer this is a great way to gauge a candidate's experience. Some developers will often just use the technologies put in front of them and neither understand nor care why. This should send up a big red flag. Being a java developer is about much more than knowing the syntax. You need to understand why systems are put together the way they are and what the pros and cons are. I expect this from candidates irrelevant of their experience. It also doesn't matter whether you were involved in architecting the system or not. You should be able to take a view on the decisions made, whether it's positive or negative. Remember, the architecture of the system itself is not on trial; if you think it's terrible then you can say as much. Very few people get to work on true greenfield projects and build their solutions up from the start, and in reality every system is going to have flaws; and that's ok. The important thing is that you know the weaknesses in your system and you can explain how you would do things differently.

Take advantage of the opportunity

If you are lucky enough to get this question then seize the chance with both hands. More than any other part of an interview this gives you the opportunity to step up and show yourself as an excellent candidate. If you can crush it then you're well on your way to a job offer.

Preparation

Sit down with a pen and a piece of paper and draw your system out. If you think the system you're working on currently isn't interesting then use something else you've worked on in the past. As a rule of thumb the interviewer shouldn't care specifically about the project you're working on right now, they just want you to talk them through a system.

Draw the relevant components. What languages are they written in and what technologies or are frameworks used? Do you agree with those choices or do you wish there was something different?

Draw and label the communications between them. Does it use files? Bus? Sockets? Pigeons? Write it down. Now explain exactly why each thing does what it does. Why was it chosen? It doesn't matter whether you were involved in the decision, or if you agree with it. Explain the reasoning (or what you think the reasoning was), and outline if this is a good or a bad thing.

If you have a way you would prefer to do it, then say that as well. Most choices in reality boil down to some sort of non functional requirement. "This is very latency sensitive so we chose this middleware to fit that requirement". "The traders don't really care so we made this a batch process as it's easier to support". Your job with this questions is to show that you understand the requirements of each component and how that relates to the technology choices. Don't forget that requirements are never purely functional. How do you support the application? What is the mean time to recovery? Is the system global or local? What happens if your datacenter floods?

Example Interview

This interview is fictional, but should be representative of what you could expect in a real interview. Apply this sort of questioning to your own system.

Can you please tell me about your system?

Sure. It takes a bunch of transaction data from downstream systems and stores it. It performs some complex transformation on it and makes it available for end users and further up stream systems to use.

Ok, could you draw it for me please?

Sure. So first of all we have the importer. This slurps in the data from a bunch of our downstream systems which have information about orders and reporting in. It's written in Java. It takes files once a day from 3 systems, and also has the option to manually import data using some web screens we threw together.

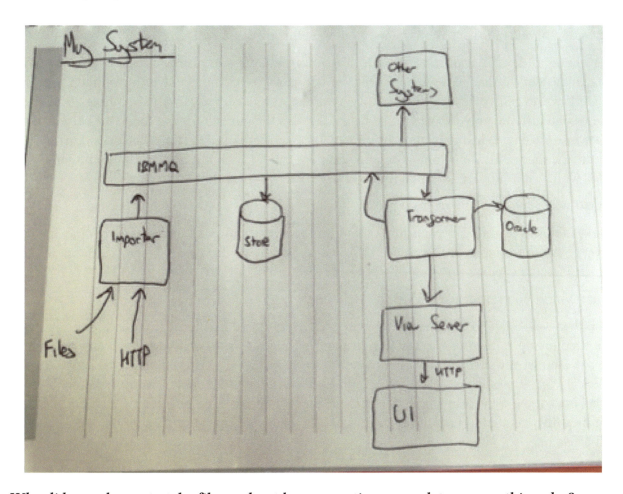

Why did you choose to take files and not have a continuous update or something else?

Legacy reasons. These systems were built many years ago and there's a reluctance to invest any money in them as they basically work. This limits us as we can't create things like customer reports in real time, only once a day. We are currently mid way through a transformational project to allow real time flows; although some systems will never be upgraded there are some brand new downstreams that need to move onto our system and want a real time interface. That's the bulk of my current job. The target state is to have a real time flow of data so that the business can see the orders as soon as they're put in. I've put an HTTP interface in there to allow intraday updates as a tactical fix. That won't cope with the data loads we're targeting but we haven't concluded how yet.

Ok, and is this system global?

Yes, we have an importer in New York and London. The systems in each are slightly different in each region so we've had to tweak the code slightly.

Do you have 1 code base then or multiple?

We used to have multiple code bases. It was a nightmare patching fixes across them so we've recently merged into a single GIT repo and we've added feature toggles based on each location. I really enjoyed learning GIT, it's much better than SVN, and it was nice to put feature toggles into practice.

And what about failover? What happens if something goes down?

To be honest it doesn't happen very often, but until recently there was no failover. As it's currently a batch system this has never been a problem but as we're trying to move to realtime updates it means if we do get problems we get very angry users. As a result we've started running 2 instances. The second instance only exposes the real time features though and doesn't touch the batches. This is because we'd have had to introduce complex failover mechanics to stop 2 batches occurring. It's a cost/risk analysis; if something goes wrong with a batch it's ok if it's delayed for a bit whilst we fix it, which isn't the case with real time.

Ok, so what does the importer do then?

It takes the files and updates and turns them into messages and puts them on our global bus. We have a bunch of components that need this data so hang it off this bus. It's using IBMMQ: not my choice, it's mandated by the company.

What would you rather use? Why choose a bus?

I'd rather use ActiveMQ. It's much easier for testing and I've had great experience with it when I've used it before. The bus was my idea. It removes a lot of issues with regards to failover. Before we had a massive web of point to point connections which were difficult to manage from a support perspective and meant that if a single component went down the system would collapse. Having a bus breaks the tight coupling between components and has seen our overall stability increase significantly; we used to have 1 outage a month last year but since introducing this we've had no full blackouts.

Are there any issues using a bus?

It's extra middleware which can be a nightmare to manage, particularly if you have a centralised team like we do. It also decreases the visibility of what's going on. We had some problems with messages going missing and had to very quickly become experts at config tuning. I think overall it was a good choice though.

Do you know any other Bus technologies?

There's HornetQ and ZeroMQ. I've not had chance to play with them but I hear HornetQ is really fast.

What format do you put on the wire?

We're using XML. I wanted to use JSON but there was push back from the upstream teams. JSON is much nicer, it's more readable, it's much less verbose and so smaller and quicker on the wire. However the other teams are heavily invested in XML so we compromised.

Ok. What next?

We have a database that hangs off that records all the data imported onto the bus. We need a historical record of data so this stores it for up to 7 years. It's a basic MySQL instance.

Why did you choose to hang it on the bus? Why not have it attached to the importer? Couldn't you have a case where the bus collapses and you'll lose a message?

We make sure to log stuff as it comes through the importer so we can manually reconcile messages in a worst case scenario. If we had to do a DB transaction every new record it would be really slow in the importer. We felt it was best to decouple this completely. It also made failover easier, as the importers just need to worry about who's publishing to the bus, and don't need to mess around with database connections.

Some of our upstreams consume this raw feed, but for others we have an enhanced feed. This transformer enriches the data with some information from a different database and puts it back onto the bus.

How quick is that?

Not very, it takes a few seconds. Right now that's not a problem but as we move to real time it needs to be fixed. I'd like to look at some near caching technologies for it.

We also have a set of user screens that feed off the data. This talks directly to the transformer.

Why did you choose to directly connect it and not use the bus?

It's another piece of legacy we haven't gotten around to fixing. Ideally it would hang off the bus too but for now it has a direct connection.

What connection are you using between them?

Plain sockets. We've got an embedded Netty server in the transformer. I'm a big fan of Netty.

What about failover?

We run the transformers in London only, but we run them hot warm. We have some basic heartbeating on the bus so they know which is alive. If the heartbeats stop then the secondary takes over.

Have you had any issues with this? What about split brain?

Yes, we've had split brain happen a couple of times. We were too aggressive with the heartbeat timeout so we've pushed that back. It's an acceptable compromise; if the transformer gets delayed for a few seconds during failover it's ok.

Hopefully you get the idea. For every system you need to be able to explain

- The technology choice
- The failover strategy
- The transport choice

You also can use this as an opportunity to express you knowledge of other technologies. In the interview there's references to Netty, ZeroMQ, HornetQ, IBMMQ, ActiveMQ, Git, Feature Toggles, heartbeating, XML vs JSON, MySQL and Oracle. That's a lot of technologies and design patterns.

This is an effective way to show that you have a broad knowledge of your domain. It's impossible to know everything which is why when hiring it's good to look for people who can introduce new ideas and technologies into the organisation. And if you don't know any then spend the time to look on google. Type in "Alternatives to " and the technology and you'll have a ton of articles laying the arguments out for you.

Core Java review

Now you're fully equipped to excel at the softer skills of interviewing it's time to learn how to answer the technical stuff. There is an unlimited selection of questions which an interviewer could ask you; the Java universe is huge. So where do you start?

The traditional method is to google around for lists of interview questions (that may even be how you found this book). The simple fact is that generally the questions will be much more in-depth than what most of what you will find- you're never going to get asked a simple list of questions. You really need to understand the areas you're talking about. That's what this section will give you; an in depth revision guide to the core areas of Java that you need to know for most interviews.

Read this half all the way through, then come back to the sections you feel you really struggle with. It's great if you can remember the esoteric facts, but you really want to concentrate on the areas you feel are your weakest. Perhaps you've never worked on a highly multi-threaded application. In that case, spend the time re-reading about Threading. Come up with practical coding examples; nothing helps lock it into memory like actually coding a solution!

Object oriented programming

Basics

Questions on object oriented programming (OOP) are exceptionally common on interviews and with good reasons. For junior developers it can clearly differentiate between someone who doesn't really understand programming and a candidate who could be a potential star but simply lacks in experience. For more senior candidates I find it can help to identify developers who understand good design and how code should be put together. There is a huge array of questions (pun intended) and it is well worth significant study. Fundamentally you will understand all of the topics covered in this chapter from the work you do in your day to day job; however being able to code away on your machine and being able to explain the concepts are very different things. We all know (hopefully) that we should aim for low coupling and high cohesion. But can you explain what that means? Can you give a concise answer? Take the time to really think about the questions below. Often answers will vary based on personal preference and experience. That's fine, as long as you have a convincing answer!

Q: Java is an object oriented language. What does that mean?

There are a number of different programming paradigms of which OOP is but one. Another would be functional programming (which is becoming very popular with languages like Scala). Programs are modelled as objects which are analogous to real world objects. For example, when modelling a car you could create a Car object, which would possess 4 Wheel objects and an Engine object. An object is defined by the data it contains and the actions that can be performed on it or with it. The four key principles of OOP are Abstraction, Encapsulation, Inheritance and Polymorphism.

Q: What is a class? What is an object?

A class can be thought of like a template; it defines what an object will look like, specifically what fields and methods it will contain. An object is said to be an instance of a class- where the fields will contain data. For example, a "TShirt" class may have a colour and size attribute. A T-Shirt object could have the colour red and the size XL. There could be many instances of an object with different or identical values for the fields.

Q: Explain Abstraction, Encapsulation, Inheritance and Polymorphism

One of the key features of Java is the idea of abstraction and inheritance. Inheritance allows the creation of a class which will have the same fields and methods of another class (and possibly more), and also be considered of the same type. For example, a Car has four wheels and an engine. Using inheritance we can create a TeslaCar, which is still a Car but also has extra fields (such as a cool touchscreen), or a FormulaOneCar, which would also be a car but have an extra field for it's spoiler. This allows us two special features: - If I have a list of cars and I want to see what colour each one is, I don't care if it's a TeslaCar or a ForumlaOneCar. I just want to call the Car's ".colour()" method. Because TeslaCar "is-a" Car, we know that it has this method available on it. - If the class we are inheriting from already has the implementation of the method, we do not need to write it ourselves (although we can if we want to).

The ability to define or override a methods implementation in a subclass results in Polymorphism. When executing a method the implementation used is not the one specified by the variable type but that of the variable instance.

```
1    public static void main(String[] args) {
2        NumberPrinter numberPrinter = new EvenNumberPrinter();
3        numberPrinter.printSomeNumbers();
4      }
5
6    private static class EvenNumberPrinter extends NumberPrinter {
7        public void printSomeNumbers() {
8            System.out.println("2468");
9          }
10      }
11
12     private static class NumberPrinter {
13         public void printSomeNumbers() {
14             System.out.println("123456");
15           }
16       }
```

This would print out "2468" despite the type being a NumberPrinter type.

This is also a good example of method overriding, where a subclass provides a different implementation to that of it's superclass. It is possible to call non-abstract methods on the super type using the keyword super, e.g. from EvenNumberPrinterâ€™s printSomeNumbers() it would be ok to call super.printSomeNumbers():

```
1    public void printSomeNumbers() {
2        super.printSomeNumbers();
3        System.out.println("2468");
4      }
```

This would result in

1   123456
2   2468

An Interface is a class with no implementation. To continue our analogy, if Car was an interface with the method .colour(), that is simply specifying that all Cars will have a colour() method (and makes no statement about how it will be implemented). You cannot create an object from an interface as it has no implementation or fields.

An abstract class is another type of class. It may have some methods which have not been implemented (which will be labelled abstract), but it may also have some methods which have been implemented. Abstract classes also cannot be used to create an object, as some implementation code will be missing.

An object can only be instantiated based on a full class (e.g. not abstract, not an interface). In Java, a class can implement between zero or many interfaces, or it can extend zero or one abstract or concrete classes only.

Encapsulation is the principal of data hiding. An object has internal state that it does not want modifying by other objects, so it can hide this. The only properties and behaviours that can be accessed on an object are those that are deliberately exposed by it's creator. This is accomplished in Java using access modifiers; public, protected, private and default.

Q: What are the different access modifiers in Java and what do they mean?

- public: accessible to everyone in the JVM
- private: only accessible from inside the class.
- protected: accessible by any class in the same package or any subclass in any package
- default: when no visibility modifier is present. accessible from any class in the same package only.

Q: What is meant when it is said we favour low coupling and high cohesion?

This is one of the key design principals in OOP. Low coupling refers to how different components interact; that could be objects, modules, systems, any level. We want components to have a very limited dependency on other components. This makes it quick and cheap to refactor and make changes to. This is usually accomplished by creating clean interfaces between components and using encapsulation to hide the internal implementation. Low coupling is one of the most important ideas for creating systems that are flexible and manageable.

Cohesion refers to the implementation of the components; in a highly cohesive system things are built in such a way that related items are put together and unrelated ones are separate. To return to the Car analogy, it makes sense that the methods for driving a car such as turn(), accelerate() and brake() exist on Car. They are cohesive and belong together. On the other hand, if the Car had a clean() method on it that would not be cohesive. A car doesn't clean itself; that is done by something else, perhaps a CarWash or an Owner. High Cohesion is achieved by ensuring that fields and behaviours that don't belong together are separated to a better place.

These terms are often referred to together because cohesive systems with low coupling tend to be more flexible and maintainable.

Q: What is the difference between method overloading and method overriding?

In Java, it is possible for multiple methods to have the same name. They are differentiated by having a different number, type and/or ordering of parameters. This is known as method overloading.

Overriding is the creation of a different implementation of a method in a subclass.

Q: What is a constructor?

A constructor is a special method which is named identical to the class, e.g. a Car class will have a constructor called Car(). A constructor does not specify a return type as it implicitly returns an object of the type of that class, in this case a Car object. It is used to build an instance of that class. If one is not specified there will be a default public no-arg constructor provided. It is possible to overload constructors, and all the access modifiers can be applied to a constructor.

If your class contains any final fields they must be assigned a value by the end of the constructor or your program will not compile.

Q: What is static in Java?

Using the static keyword effectively declares that something belongs to the class, not to the object instance. The static variable is shared by all instances of the object. A static method belongs to the class, meaning that it cannot access any non-static field values. It also means it cannot be overridden. We can also have static code blocks which are executed when a class is loaded into memory:

```
1  static{
2      System.out.println("Hello!");
3      //maybe initialise some static variables here
4  }
```

Static can also be used for nested classes.

Q: What does it mean when we say java does not support multiple inheritance? Is this a good thing?

Java cannot extend functionality from more than one concrete or abstract class. If both parent classes had a jump() method, it would be unclear which functionality the caller would need to use. We can implement multiple interfaces however as the the implementation occurs in our actual class so this problem does not occur.

Q: If you wanted to prevent your methods or classes from being overridden, how would you do this?

By declaring something as final you prevent it from being overridden. Nothing is perfect though, as crafty developers can always use Reflection to get around this, or alternatively just copy and paste your code into their own version of the class. It is rarely a good idea to prevent your methods or classes being overridden, and you should code defensively to reflect this.

Data structures

Java data structures interview questions will come up in your interview. At it's nexus being a programmer is about handling data, transforming and outputting it from one format to another, which is why it is so important to understand what's going on under the hood and how it can affect your application. It never fails to confound me how many people can't tell what collection is used to back an ArrayList (hint: it's in the name). From the interviewer's perspective, questions on data structures reveal a lot of information about the candidate. They show if the candidate has a core understanding of how java works. Even better it provides a platform to lead to a wide ranging set of questions on design, algorithms and a whole lot more. In day to day java programming, you're going to spend most of your time with ArrayLists, LinkedLists and HashMaps. As a result it makes sense to review collections and algorithms you haven't looked at for a while as, in my experience, companies love asking this sort of question.

- Q: What is the Java Collection Framework?
- Q: What Collection types are there in Java?
- Q: What are the basic interface types?
- Q: What are the differences between List, Set and Map?

This is the bread and butter stuff that everyone who uses Java should know. The collections framework is simply the set of collection types that are included as part of core java. There are three types of collection you will deal with in Java; Set and List (both of which implement Collection) and Maps (which implement Map and technically aren't part of core Collections). Each type of collection exhibits certain characteristics which define it's usage. The key features of a collection are:

- Elements can be added or removed
- The collection will have a size that can be queried
- The collection may or may not contain duplicates
- It may or may not provide ordering
- It may or may not provide positional access (e.g. get me item at location 6)

The behaviour of these methods varies based on implementation (as you would expect from an interface). What happens on if you call *remove()* on a collection for an object that doesn't exist? It depends on the implementation.

The collection types

Set: A set has no duplicates and no guaranteed order. Because of this, it does not provide positional access. Implements Collection. Example implementations include TreeSet and HashSet.

List: A list may or may not contain duplicates and also guarantees order, allowing positional access. Implements Collection. Example implementations include ArrayList and LinkedList.

Map: A map is slightly different as it contains key-value pairs as opposed to specific object. The key of a map may not contain duplicates. A map has no guaranteed order and no positional access. Does not implement Collection. Example implementations include HashMap and TreeMap.

But what does this mean with regards to interviews? You're almost certainly going to get a question about the differences between the types so make an effort to learn them. More importantly the smart interviewee understands what the implication of these features are. Why would you choose one over the other? What are the implications?

Which to choose?

In reality, whether you choose a Set, List or Map will depend on the structure of your data. If you won't have duplicates and you don't need order, then your choice will lie with a set. If you need to enshrine order into your data, then you will choose List. If you have key-value pairs, usually if you want to associate two different objects or an object has an obvious identifier, then you will want to choose a map.

Examples

- A collection of colours would be best put into a set. There is no ordering to the elements, and there are no duplicates; You can't have two copies of "Red"!
- The batting order of a cricket team would be good to put in a list; you want to retain the order of the objects.
- A collection of web sessions would be best in a map; the unique session ID would make a good key/reference to the real object.

Understanding why you choose a collection is vitally important for giving the best impression in interviews. I've had candidates come in and tell me they just use ArrayList and HashMap because that's just the default implementation they choose to use. In reality, this maybe isn't a bad thing. Most times we need to use collections there are no major latency or access requirements. It doesn't matter. However, people who are asking you these questions in interviews want to know that you understand how things work under the covers.

Q: What are the main concerns when choosing a collection?

When you're handling a collection, you care about speed, specifically

- Speed of access
- Speed of adding a new element
- Speed of removing an element
- Speed of iteration

On top of this, it isn't just a case of "which is faster". There is also consistency. Some implementations will guarantee the speed of access, whereas others will have variable speed. How that speed is determined depends on the implementation. The important thing to understand is the speed of the relative collection implementations to each other, and how that influences your selection.

Collection implementations

- Q: Why would I choose LinkedList over an ArrayList?
- Q: Which is faster, TreeSet or HashSet?
- Q: How does a LinkedList work?

The collection implementations tend to be based on either a *Linked* implementation, a *Tree* implementation or a *Hash* implementation. There are entire textbooks based on this, but what you need to know is how it affects your collection choices.

Linked implementation

Example: LinkedList, LinkedHashSet Under the covers, each item is held in a "node". Each node has a pointer to the next item in the collection like so.

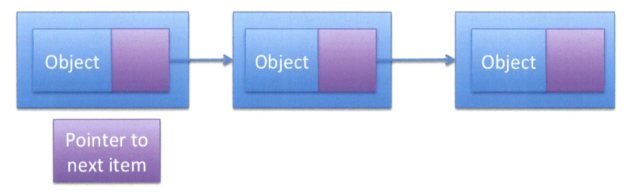

What does this mean for speed?

When adding an item into a linked connection it's quick, irrelevant of where you're adding the node. If you have a list of 3 items and want to add a new one in position 1, the operation is simply to point position 2 to the new item, and the new item to the old position 2.

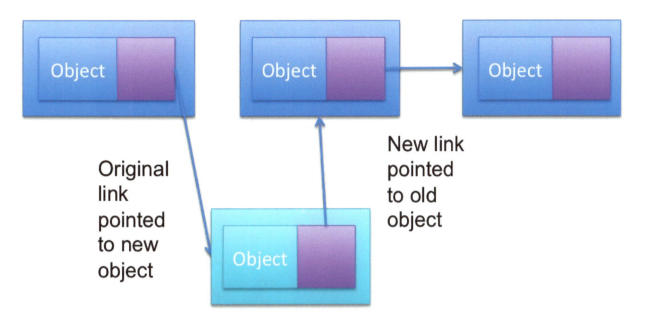

That's pretty fast! No copying collections, no moving things, no reordering. The same is true for removals; simply point node 0 to node 2 and you've removed node 1.

Conversely when accessing objects it is relatively slow. If you have a list of 1000 items, and you want item 999, you need to traverse every single node to get to that item. This also means that the access speed is not consistent. It's quicker to access element 1 than it is element 1000. Bear in mind that when adding a new object you need to first traverse to the node before, so this can have some impact on speed.

So linked collections such as LinkedList are great when you need fast addition/removal and access time is less of a concern. **If you're going to be adding/remove items from your collection a lot, then this is the option for you.**

Array implementation

Example: ArrayList. ArrayList is the only Array based implementation in the collection classes, but is often used to compare to LinkedList so it's important to understand. As alluded to previously, ArrayLists are backed by an Array. This has interesting implications.

When adding an item into the middle of an ArrayList, the structure needs to copy all of the items to shift them down the Array. This can be slow, and is not guaranteed time (depending on how many elements need to be copied.

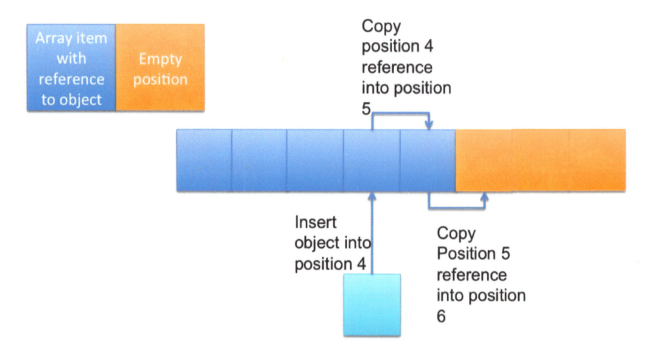

The same applies when removing objects; all object references after it have to be copied forward one space. There is an even worse case. On creating an ArrayList it starts with a fixed length Array (whose length you can set in the constructor, or the default is 10). If the capacity needs to increase over this, the collection has to create a **brand new array** of greater length and copy all the references to it which can be really slow.

Where ArrayList succeeds is access speed; as the array is in contiguous memory it means that if you request object 999 of 1000, you can calculate exactly where in memory the reference is with no need to traverse the full collection. This gives constant time access which is **fast**.

So, ArrayLists make a great choice if you have a set of data that is **unlikely to be modified significantly, and you need speedy read access.**

Hash implementation

Examples: HashSet, HashMap. The HashMap is a complicated beast in itself and is a good choice for an interview question as it is easy to add extending questions to.

Q: **How does a HashMap work?**

Q: **Why does the hashcode of the key matter?**

Q: **What happens if two objects have the same HashCode?**

Q: **How does the Map select the correct object if there is a clash?**

Interestingly HashSet is backed by HashMap, so for the purpose of this I will just discuss the latter. A HashMap works like this: under the covers a HashMap is an array of references (called the Entry

Table, which defaults to 16 entries) to a group of LinkedLists (called Buckets) where HashEntries are stored. A HashEntry is an object containing the key and associated object.

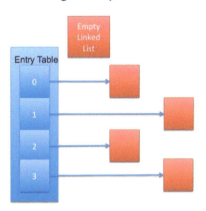

All instances of Object have a method, hashCode(), which returns an int. The hashcode is usually a value derived from the properties of an object. The hashcode returned from an object should be consistent and equal objects must return the same hashcode. This property can then be used to determine which bucket to put it in based on the index of the entry table; for example, in the above example with 4 spaces in the entry table, if I have a key in with HashCode 123456, I can do 12345 % 4 = 1, so I would place my object in bucket 1.

This makes object retrieval very quick. In my example, if I try to retrieve the object for my key then all I need to do is the same mod calculation to find the bucket and it's the first entry. Exceptionally quick.

This can get more complicated. What if I have two more objects, HashCode of "5" and "9"? They both have a (modulus 4) of 1 so would both be put into bucket 1 too. Now when I use my "9" key to retrieve my object the HashMap has to iterate through a LinkedList, calling .equals() on the keys of each HashEntry.

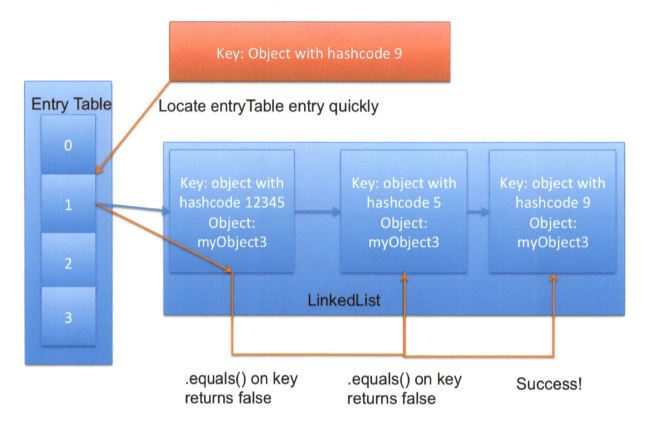

This is slow! Fortunately, this shouldn't happen often. Although collisions will naturally occur, the intention is that objects will be spread evenly across the entry table with minimal collisions. This relies on a well implemented hashcode function. If the hashcode is poor (e.g., always return 0) then you will hit collisions.

To further try and reduce the chance of this, each HashMap has a load factor (which defaults to 0.75). If the entry table is more full than the load factor (e.g. if more than 75% of the entry table has entries) then, similar to the ArrayList, the HashMap will double the size of the entry table and reorder the entries. This is known as rehashing.

Tree implementation

Examples: TreeMap, TreeSet. The Tree implementation is completely different to any of the data structures we've considered before and is considerably more complicated. It is based on a Red Black tree, a complicated algorithm which you're unlikely to get asked about (if you're really keen then watch http://www.csanimated.com/animation.php?t=Red-black_tree). Values are stored in an ordered way, determined either by the natural ordering of the object or using a **Comparator** passed in as part of the constructor. This means on all implementations the collection will re-sort itself to maintain this natural order. When retrieving items it is necessary to navigate the tree, potentially traversing a large number of nodes for sizeable collections. The important thing to note from your perspective: **this is slower than HashMap.** Considerably slower. If speed is the goal then always use a HashMap or HashSet. However, if ordering is important then TreeMap/TreeSet should be your collection of choice.

Multithreading and collections

Collections and Threading are intrinsically linked; many of the core problems related to Threading are regarding shared data access. How can we access data from multiple threads in a fast yet safe fashion?

How do I create a Thread Safe collection?

The easiest way to make something threadsafe if to make it immutable. An immutable object is one whose state cannot be altered. If it cannot change then it is safe for all threads to read it without any problems. This can be achieved in Java using the Collections.unmodifiable methods.

```
1   Collections.unmodifiableCollection
2   Collections.unmodifiableSet
3   Collections.unmodifiableSortedSet
4   Collections.unmodifiableList
5   Collections.unmodifiableCollection
6   Collections.unmodifiableMap
7   Collections.unmodifiableSortedMap
```

All of these collections act as a wrapper around a standard collection and guarantee access safety; any attempts to modify the collection will result in an UnsupportedOperationException. However, this is only a *view* on the data. If everyone is accessing via the unmodifiable version, then this is thread safe; however the underlying collection could still change. For example:

```
1   LinkedList<String> words = new LinkedList<>();
2   words.add("Hello");
3   words.add("There");
4   List<String> unmodifiableList = Collections.unmodifiableList(words);
5   System.out.println(unmodifiableList);
6   words.add("Cheating");
7   System.out.println(unmodifiableList);
8   //result:
9   //[Hello, There]
10  //[Hello, There, Cheating]
```

As a result this isn't really immutable. Such things as a truly ImmutableList do exist in third party libraries such as Google Guava, but not in the core language. It's also important to note that immutable collections don't normally satisfy the needs of our programs; often data needs to be written and read, so we need a bigger solution.

In Java 5, the java.util.concurrent package was introduced with the specific aim of making life easier for dealing with collections in a thread safe way.

Q: Tell me about the java.util.concurrent package that was introduced in Java 5. Why is it important? Why does it matter?

The guys who write Java are smarter than you or me (or they should be). Instead of everyone having to write their own implementation to ensure thread safety, making sure the right things were locked in the right places without destroying performance, java.util.concurrent provides a number of collection types which guarantee thread safety with the minimum performance impact.

It also introduced a bunch of other cool Thread related features, which will be covered in the Threading chapter.

The queues

- ConcurrentLinkedDeque
- ConcurrentLinkedQueue
- LinkedBlockingQueue
- LinkedBlockingDeque
- LinkedTransferQueue
- PriorityBlockingQueue
- ArrayBlockingQueue

That's a lot of queues (and double ended queues, a deque)! The key things to note:

- A Blocking queue will block a consumer/producer when the queue is empty/full. This is a necessary mechanism to allow a producer/consumer pattern. The BlockingQueue interface has put() and take() methods to allow for this.
- A Transfer queue is a blocking queue, with extra methods to allow a consumer to wait for a message to be consumed.
- A Priority queue will order elements based on their natural ordering or using a comparator passed in at construction time.

All of the implementations use Compare and Set (CAS) operations, not synchronized blocks to ensure thread safety. This ensures no risk of deadlock and Threads do not get stuck waiting, and is also significantly faster. All collections based on CAS operations, such as the above, have weakly consistent iterators. This means that they will not throw ConcurrentModificationExceptions but they make no guarantee to reflect the correct state; from the documentation:

The returned iterator is a "weakly consistent" iterator that will never throw ConcurrentModification-Exception and guarantees to traverse elements as they existed upon construction of the iterator, and may (but is not guaranteed to) reflect any modifications subsequent to construction.

The CopyOnWrites

Q: How can ConcurrentModificationException be avoided when iterating a collection?

- CopyOnWriteArrayList
- CopyOnWriteArraySet

I'm a big fan of well named Classes, and this is a great example. By copying the entire collection on every write it guarantees immutability; if I have an iterator looping through a collection then it can guarantee that the collection will not be modified as it is being traversed as all modifications will result in a copy of the data being created. This can be an expensive operation so these collections lend themselves better to data that has frequent access but infrequent update. An iterator which relies on the data being copied, such as in this case, is known as a fail safe iterator.

ConcurrentHashMap

Q: How is ConcurrentHashMap implemented?

ConcurrentHashMap is a highly efficient, thread safe implementation of HashMap. As discussed earlier, a HashMap is made up of segments, a number of lists (defaulting to 16) which contain the data which are accessed based on HashCode. In ConcurrentHashMap read operations are generally not blocking which allows for it to be very speedy; writes only block by segment. This means that the other 15 segments can be read without issue if an update is being written.

Q: Should I use a HashTable or a ConcurrentHashMap?

HashTable is a synchronized implementation of HashMap but it is from an old version of Java and should no longer be used. All operations are synchronized in HashTable which means it's performance is very poor relative to ConcurrentHashMap.

Q: Are collections such as ConccurrentLinkedQueue and ConcurrentHashMap completely Thread safe?

The answer is both yes and no. The implementation is completely ThreadSafe and can be used as a replacement for their non Thread safe counterparts. However, it is very possible to write code which access the collection in a non Thread safe manner.

```
1  Map<String, String> map = new ConcurrentHashMap<>();
2  map.put("a", "1");
3  map.put("b", "2");
4  //....Set off a bunch of other threads....
5  if (!map.containsKey("c"))
6      map.put("c", "3");
7  else
8      map.get("c");
```

The contains -> put and contains -> get operations are not atomic. Between checking for existence and putting/getting anything can happen in the collection. The collection is still thread safe, our access simply isn't. We need to ensure any operations where we check state and then execute are done in an atomic or synchronized way. The above code could be rectified by making use of the putIfAbsent method to create atomicity; however if for example you wanted to perform an action to a list based on it's size you may need to lock the collection to ensure it happens as a single operation.

Java exceptions

Java exceptions are one of my favourite questions to ask during telephone interviews. They're one of the simpler parts of Java so I would expect most candidates to be able to give good answers. It's normally easy to weed out those who don't as not worth my time. However what I really like about exceptions as interview fodder is that they allow the combination of a technical core java question with an opinion piece. Checked exceptions are actually a really controversial part of Java and it's good to see which side of the fence a candidate falls on, or whether they are even aware that the fence is there.

Core questions

Q: What is an Exception in Java?

I don't normally ask this question as it's so basic but it's good to make sure you've got a standard answer in your pocket. Exceptions are a way to programmatically convey system and programming errors. All exceptions inherit from Throwable. When something goes wrong you can use the throw keyword to fire an exception.

Q: There are 2 types of exception in Java, what are they and what's the difference?

It still amazes me how much the "2 types" question throws people (yep, throws, I did it again, another pun). This is as basic as core java gets. If you don't get this then it tells me that you didn't learn core java properly (or at all) which will probably act as a shaky base for the rest of your knowledge. Get this answer right. The two types of exception are **checked** and **unchecked**. I've heard some strange answers in my time including "Runtime and NullPointerException"! A checked exception is one that forces you to catch it. It forms part of the API or contract. Anyone using code that throws a checked exception can see that as it is declared on the method and they are forced to handle it using a try/catch block. Unchecked exceptions do not need to be caught and do not notify anyone using the code that it could be thrown.

Q: How do I know if an Exception class is checked or unchecked?

All exceptions are checked exceptions except those that inherit from java.lang.RuntimeException.

Q: What does "finally" do?

Exceptions are caught using a try-catch block. However following the catch you can have a finally block. This block is guaranteed to execute no matter what happens (short of someone pulling out the plug), such as if an exception is thrown in the catch block. This is really useful to ensure the clean up of resources such as Connections.

Q: Can I throw multiple exceptions from the same method? How do I catch them?

Yes you can, each exception (or a parent of that class) just need listing after the "throws" in the method signature. You can catch them using multiple catch blocks, or by catching a parent exception class e.g. you can just catch Exception which will catch all exceptions. This is in theory bad practice as you lose the nuance of what went wrong and specifically the ability to recover. You can also catch multiple exceptions in a single catch block as of Java 7. When catching exceptions it is important to do so in order from **most specific** to **least specific**. If your catch block catches Exception first and then IOException second, the first catch block will always catch any exception coming through and the IOException will be rendered useless (and in fact it will cause a compiler error saying the exception has already been caught.)

Q: What do you think of Checked Exceptions, are they a good thing?

Q: When you're writing your own code and you need to throw a custom exception, do you create a checked or unchecked exception?

Q: C# does not have checked exceptions. Can you tell me why this might be? Who do you think was right, Java or C sharp?

I love these questions so much. It's a really good way to stretch a candidate and to see if they understand how to architect systems. Having an appropriate policy on exceptions is key to maintaining a clean code base, and you'll quickly figure out who's thought about the issue and who hasn't. A must read before your interview is this interview with the creator of C# on why he didn't include checked exceptions in the language.[2] The argument in general is that checked exceptions cause ugly code in Java. Handling is incredibly verbose, and normally most developers don't know how to handle them or are too lazy to. This results in empty catch blocks or just log statements. This results in a brittle system where exceptions get swallowed never to be heard from again and the system can get into a brittle state without telling anyone. On the positive side for checked, it declares on the API what it's going to do so consumers can handle it. This is good if you're handing out a library. However a lot of developers use this for evil, and control the flow of their system using exceptions. Exceptions are for exceptional circumstances only.

As with most discussion questions the important part is not that the developer agrees with your opinion but that they are capable of forming an opinion and explaining it. I personally fall heavily on the side that checked exceptions are terrible and developers misuse them. In my code all checked exceptions get wrapped in an application specific RuntimeException and thrown up the stack where I'll normally have an exception guard to catch and log the issue. However if a candidate says they use checked exceptions in their code and can explain why with an understanding of the problems then they get a pass. Just make sure you've thought about where you lie on the issue before you go in for your interview so you can articulate it to the interviewer. And if you've never thought about it before, then remember checked exceptions are evil :).

---

[2] http://www.artima.com/intv/handcuffs.html

JVM and garbage collection

The Java Virtual Machine is the achilles heel of most developers and can cause even the most seasoned developers to come unstuck. The simple fact is that unless something is going wrong, we don't normally care about it. Maybe we tune it a little when the application goes live but after that it remains untouched until something goes wrong. This makes it a very difficult subject to excel in during interviews. Even worse, interviewers love to ask questions about it. Everyone should have a basic knowledge of the JVM to be able to do their job but often people recruiting are looking for someone who knows how to fix a problem like a memory leak when it happens.

In this guide we take a ground up approach to the JVM and garbage collection so you can feel some level of confidence going into your big day.

Q: What is the JVM? Why is it a good thing? What is "write once, run anywhere"? Are there negatives?

JVM stands for Java Virtual Machine. Java code is compiled down into an intermediary language called byte code. The Java Virtual Machine is then responsible for executing this byte code. This is unlike languages such as C++ which are compiled directly to native code for a specific platform.

This is what gives Java its 'write once, run anywhere' ability. In a language which compiles directly to native you would have to compile and test the application separately on every platform on which you wish it to run. There would likely be several issues with libraries, ensuring they are available on all of the platforms for example. Every new platform would require new compilation and new testing. This is time consuming and expensive.

On the other hand a java program can be run on any system where a Java Virtual Machine is available. The JVM acts as the intermediary layer and handles the OS specific details which means that as developers we shouldn't need to worry about it. In reality there are still some kinks between different operating systems, but these are relatively small. This makes it quicker and easier to develop, and means developers can write software on windows laptops that may be destined for other platforms. I only need to write my software once and it is available on a huge variety of platforms, from Android to Solaris.

In theory this is at the cost of speed. The extra layer of the JVM means it is slower than direct-to-tin languages like C. However java has been making a lot of progress in recent years, and given the many other benefits such as ease of use, it is being used more and more often for low latency applications.

The other benefit of the JVM is that any language that can compile down to byte code can run on it, not just java. Languages like Groovy, Scala and Clojure are all JVM based languages. This also means the languages can easily use libraries written in other languages. As a Scala developer I can use Java libraries in my applications as it all runs on the same platform.

The separation from the real hardware also means the code is sandboxed, limiting the amount of damage it can do to a host computer. Security is a great benefit of the JVM.

There is another interesting facet to consider; not all JVMs are built equal. There are a number of different implementations beyond the standard JVM implementation from Oracle. JRockit is renowned for being an exceptionally quick JVM. OpenJDK is an open source equivalent. There are tons of JVM implementations available. Whilst this choice is ultimately a good thing, all of the JVMs may behave slightly differently. A number of areas of the Java specification are left intentionally vague with regards to their implementation and each VM may do things differently. This can result in a bug which only manifests in a certain VM in a certain platform. These can be some of the hardest bugs to figure out.

From a developer perspective, the JVM offers a number of benefits, specifically around memory management and performance optimisation.

Q: What is JIT?

JIT stands for "Just in Time". As discussed, the JVM executes bytecode. However, if it determines a section of code is being run frequently it can optionally compile a section down to native code to increase the speed of execution. The smallest block that can be JIT compiled is a method. By default, a piece of code needs to be executed 1500 times for it to be JIT compiled although this is configurable. This leads to the concept of "warming up" the JVM. It will be at it's most performant the longer it runs as these optimisations occur. On the downside, JIT compilation is not free; it takes time and resource when it occurs.

Q: What do we mean when we say memory is managed in Java? What is the Garbage Collector?

In languages like C the developer has direct access to memory. The code references memory space addresses. This can be difficult and dangerous, and can result in damaging memory leaks. In Java all memory is managed. As a programmer we deal exclusively in objects and primitives and have no concept of what is happening underneath with regards to memory and pointers. Most importantly, Java has the concept of a garbage collector. When objects are no longer needed the JVM will automatically identify and clear the memory space for us.

Q: What are the benefits and negatives of the Garbage Collector?

On the positive side:

- The developer can worry much less about memory management and concentrate on actual problem solving. Although memory leaks are still technically possible they are much less common.
- The GC has a lot of smart algorithms for memory management which work automatically in the background. Contrary to popular belief, these can often be better at determining when best to perform GC than when collecting manually.

On the negative side

- When a garbage collection occurs it has an effect on the application performance, notably slowing it down or stopping it. In so called "Stop the world" garbage collections the rest of the application will freeze whilst this occurs. This is can be unacceptable depending on the application requirements, although GC tuning can minimise or even remove any impact.
- Although it's possible to do a lot of tuning with the garbage collector, you cannot specify when or how the application performs GC.

Q: What is "Stop the World"?

When a GC happens it is necessary to completely pause the threads in an application whilst collection occurs. This is known as Stop The World. For most applications long pauses are not acceptable. As a result it is important to tune the garbage collector to minimise the impact of collections to be acceptable for the application.

Q: How does Generational GC work? Why do we use generational GC? How is the Java Heap structured?

It is important to understand how the Java Heap works to be able to answer questions about GC. All objects are stored on the Heap (as opposed to the Stack, where variables and methods are stored along with references to objects in the heap). Garbage Collection is the process of removing objects which are no longer needed from the Heap and returning the space for general consumption. Almost all GCs are "generational", where the Heap is divided into a number of sections, or generations. This has proven significantly more optimal which is why almost all collectors use this pattern.

New generation

Q: What is the New Generation? How does it help to minimise the impact of GC?

Most applications have a high volume of short lived objects. Analyzing all objects in an application during a GC would be slow and time consuming, so it therefore makes sense to separate the shortlived objects so that they can be quickly collected. As a result all new objects are placed into the new generation. New gen is split up further:

- Eden Space: all new objects are placed in here. When it becomes full, a minor GC occurs. all objects that are still referenced are then promoted to a **survivor space**
- Survivor spaces: The implementation of survivor spaces varies based on the JVM but the premise is the same. Each GC of the New Generation increments the age of objects in the survivor space. When an object has survived a sufficient number of minor GCs (defaults vary but normally start at 15) it will then be promoted to the Old Generation. Some implementations use two survivor spaces, a From space and a To space. During each collection these will swap roles, with all promoted Eden objects and surviving objects moved to the To space, leaving From empty.

Q: What is a minor GC?

A garbage collection in the NewGen is known as a **minor GC**. One of the benefits of using a New Generation is the reduction of the impact of fragmentation. When an object is garbage collected, it leaves a gap in the memory where it was. We can compact the remaining objects (a stop-the-world scenario) or we can leave them and slot new objects in. By having a Generational GC we limit the amount that this happens in the Old Generation as it is generally more stable which is good for improving latencies by reducing stop the world. However if we do not compact we may find objects cannot just fit in the spaces inbetween, perhaps due to size concerns. If this is the case then you will see objects failing to be promoted from New Generation.

Old generation

Q: Explain what the old generation is?

Any objects that survive from survivor spaces in the New Generation are promoted to the Old Generation. The Old Generation is usually much larger than the New Generation. When a GC occurs in old gen it is known as a **full GC**. Full GCs are also stop-the-world and tend to take longer, which is why most JVM tuning occurs here. There are a number of different algorithms available for Garbage Collection, and it is possible to use different algorithms for new and old gen.

Q: What type of Garbage Collectors are there?

Serial GC

Designed when computers only had one CPU and stops the entire application whilst GC occurs. It uses **mark-sweep-compact**. The collector goes through all of the objects and marks which objects are available for Garbage Collection, before clearing them out and then copying all of the objects into contiguous space (so therefore has no fragmentation).

Parallel GC

Similar to Serial, except that it uses multiple threads to perform the GC in order to be faster.

Concurrent Mark Sweep (CMS)

CMS GC minimises pauses by doing most of the GC related work concurrently with the processing of the application. This minimises the amount of time when the application has to completely pause and so lends itself much better to applications which are sensitive to this. CMS is a non compacting algorithm which can lead to fragmentation problems. The CMS collector uses Parallel GC for the young generation.

G1GC (garbage first garbage collector)

A concurrent parallel collector that is viewed as the long term replacement for CMS and does not suffer from the same fragmentation problems as CMS.

Q: Which is better? Serial, Parallel or CMS?

It depends entirely on the application. Each one is tailored to the requirements of the application. Serial is better if you're on a single CPU, or in a scenario where there are more VMs running on the machine than CPUs. Parallel is a throughput collector and really good if you have a lot of work to do but you're ok with pauses. CMS/G1GC is the best of the options if you need consistent responsiveness with minimal pauses.

PermGen

Q: What is the PermGen?

The PermGen is where the JVM stores the metadata about classes. It no longer exists in Java 8, having been replaced with metaspace. Generally the PermGen doesn't require any tuning above ensuring it has enough space, although it is possible to have leaks if Classes are not being unloaded properly.

From the code

Q: Can you tell the system to perform a garbage collection?

This is an interesting question: the answer is both yes and no. We can use the call "System.gc()" to suggest to the JVM to perform a garbage collection. However, there is no guarantee this will do anything. As a java developer, we don't know for certain what JVM our code is being run in. The JVM spec makes no guarantees on what will happen when this method is called. There is even a startup flag, -XX:+DisableExplicitGC, which will stop this from doing anything.

It is considered bad practice to use System.gc().

Q: What does finalize() do?

finalize() is a method on java.lang.Object so exists on all objects. The default implementation does nothing. It is called by the garbage collector when it determines there are no more references to the object. As a result there are no guarantees the code will ever be executed and so should not be used to execute actual functionality. Instead it is used for clean up, such as file references. It will never be called more than once on an object (by the JVM).

JVM tuning

Q: What flags can I use to tune the JVM and GC?

There are textbooks available on tuning the JVM for optimal Garbage Collection. You'll never know them all! Nonetheless it's good to know a few for the purpose of interview.

-XX:-UseConcMarkSweepGC: Use the CMS collector for the Old Gen.

-XX:-UseParallelGC: Use Parallel GC for New Gen

-XX:-UseParallelOldGC: Use Parallel GC for Old and New Gen.

-XX:-HeapDumpOnOutOfMemoryError: Create a thread dump when the application runs out of memory. Very useful for diagnostics.

-XX:-PrintGCDetails: Log out details of Garbage Collection.

-Xms512m: Sets the initial heap size to 512m **-Xmx1024m**: Sets the maximum heap size to 1024m

-XX:NewSize and -XX:MaxNewSize: Specifically set the default and max size of the New Generation

-XX:NewRatio=3: Set the size of the Young Generation as a ratio of the size of the Old Generation.

-XX:SurvivorRatio=10: Set the size of Eden space relative to the size of a survivor space.

Diagnosis

Whilst all of the questions above are very good to know to show you have a basic understanding of how the JVM works, one of the most standard questions during an interview is this:

Have you ever experienced a memory leak? How did you diagnose it?

This is a difficult question to answer for most people as although they may have done it, chances are it was a long time ago and isn't something you can recall easily. The best way to prepare is to actually try and write an application with a memory leak and attempt to diagnosis it. Below I have created a ridiculous example of a memory leak which will allow us to go step by step through the process of identifying the problem. **I strongly advise you download the code and follow through this process.** It is much more likely to be committed to your memory if you actually do this process.

```java
import java.util.ArrayDeque;
import java.util.Deque;
public class Main {
    public static void main(String[] args) {
        TaskList taskList = new TaskList();
        final TaskCreator taskCreator = new TaskCreator(taskList);
        new Thread(new Runnable() {
            @Override
            public void run() {
                for (int i = 0; i < 100000; i++) {
                    taskCreator.createTask();
                }
            }
        }).start();
    }
    private static class TaskCreator {
```

```
17          private TaskList taskList;
18          public TaskCreator(TaskList taskList) {
19              this.taskList = taskList;
20          }
21          public void createTask() {
22              taskList.addTask(new Task());
23          }
24      }
25      private static class TaskList {
26          private Deque<Task> tasks = new ArrayDeque<Task>();
27          public void addTask(Task task) {
28              tasks.add(task);
29              tasks.peek().execute();//Memory leak!
30          }
31      }
32      private static class Task {
33          private Object[] array = new Object[1000];
34          public void execute() {
35              //dostuff
36          }
37      }
38  }
```

In the above very contrived example, the application executes tasks put onto a Deque. However when we run this we get an out of memory! What could it possibly be?

```
Exception in thread "Thread-0" java.lang.OutOfMemoryError: Java heap space
    at com.core.interview.Task.<init>(Task.java:8)
    at com.core.interview.TaskCreator.createTask(TaskCreator.java:13)
    at com.core.interview.Main$1.run(Main.java:13)
    at java.lang.Thread.run(Thread.java:722)
```

To find out we need to use a profiler. A profiler allows us to look at exactly what is going on the VM. There are a number of options available. VisualVM (https://visualvm.java.net/download.html) is free and allows basic profiling. For a more complete tool suite there are a number of options but my personal favourite is Yourkit. It has an amazing array of tools to help you with diagnosis and analysis. However the principles used are generally the same.

I started running my application locally, then fired up VisualVM and selected the process. You can then watch exactly what's going on in the heap, permgen etc.

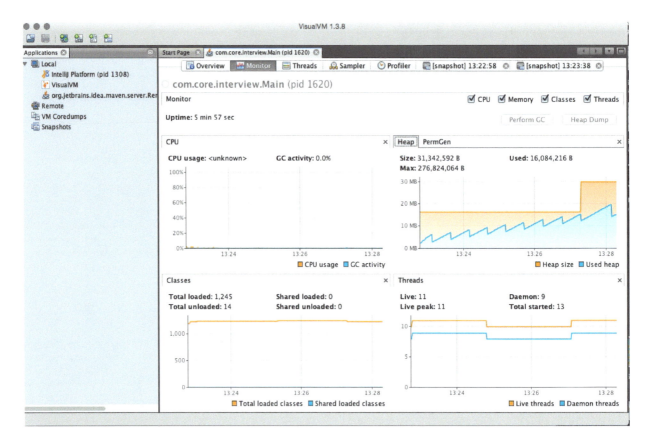

You can see on the heap (top right) the tell tail signs of a memory leak. The application sawtooths, which is not a problem per se, but the memory is consistently going up and not returning to a base level. This smells like a memory leak. But how can we tell what's going on? If we head over to the Sampler tab we can get a clear indication of what is sitting on our heap.

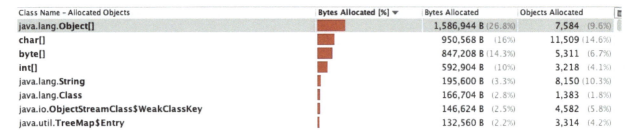

Class Name – Allocated Objects	Bytes Allocated [%] ▼	Bytes Allocated	Objects Allocated
java.lang.Object[]		1,586,944 B (26.8%)	7,584 (9.6%)
char[]		950,568 B (16%)	11,509 (14.6%)
byte[]		847,208 B (14.3%)	5,311 (6.7%)
int[]		592,904 B (10%)	3,218 (4.1%)
java.lang.String		195,600 B (3.3%)	8,150 (10.3%)
java.lang.Class		166,704 B (2.8%)	1,383 (1.8%)
java.io.ObjectStreamClass$WeakClassKey		146,624 B (2.5%)	4,582 (5.8%)
java.util.TreeMap$Entry		132,560 B (2.2%)	3,314 (4.2%)

Those Object arrays look a bit odd. But how do we know if that's the problem? Visual VM allows us to take snapshots, like a photograph of the memory at that time. The above screenshot is a snapshot from after the application had only been running for a little bit. The next snapshot a couple of minutes later confirms this:

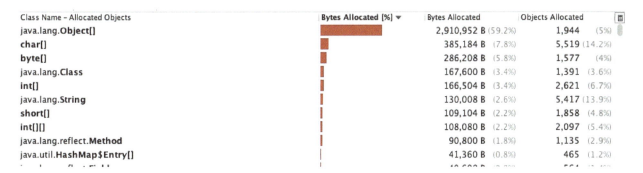

We can actually compare these directly by selecting both in the menu and selecting compare.

There's definitely something funky going on with the array of objects. How can we figure out the leak though? By using the profile tab. If I go to profile, and in settings enable "record allocations stack traces" we can then find out where the leak has come from.

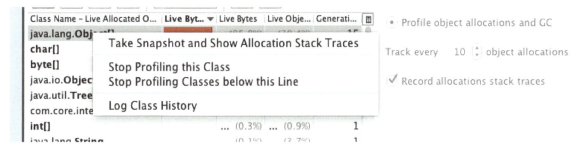

By now taking snapshot and showing allocation traces we can see where the object arrays are being instantiated.

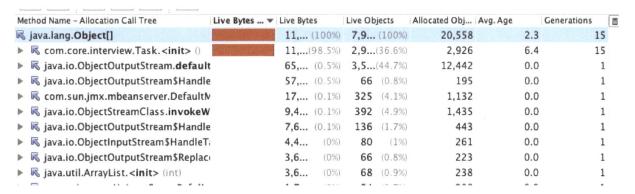

Looks like there are thousands of Task objects holding references to Object arrays! But what is holding onto these Task items?

If we go back to the "Monitor" tab we can create a heap dump. If we double click on the Object[] in the heap dump it will show us all instances in the application, and in the bottom right panel we can identify where the reference is.

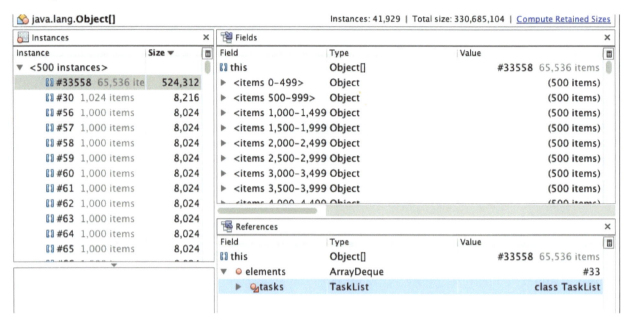

It looks like TaskList is the culprit! If we take a look at the code we can see what the problem is.

```
1   tasks.peek().execute();
```

We're never clearing the reference after we've finished with it! If we change this to use poll() then the memory leak is fixed.

Whilst clearly this is a very contrived example, going through the steps will refresh your memory for if you are asked to explain how you would identify memory leaks in an application. Look for memory continuing to increase despite GCs happening, take memory snapshot and compare them to see which Objects may be candidates for not being released, and use a heap dump to analyse what is holding references to them.

Threading

As a developer the single best thing we can do for producing clean, understandable code that won't fall over is to avoid putting any multi threading into your code base. The best programmers can break most problems down to be solved without complex threading. Poor programmers will throw threading in to fix a problem they don't understand or to prematurely optimise. Threading questions are exceptionally popular for interviews so it's important to be able to demonstrate a sound understanding of how threads work in Java, when and why we use them, and how to actually program them in a safe manner. In this article we will tackle threading from the ground up and cover what you need to know to be able to answer any questions that come up.

Introduction to threading

Q: What is a Thread?

Q: How do we create Threads in java?

Threads allow us to do more than one thing at once. Without Threads code is executed in a linear fashion, one command after another. By using threads we can perform multiple actions at the same time. This takes advantage of the fact that computers now have multiple processors as well as the ability to time slice tasks, so multiple threads can even be run on a single processors. There are 2 main ways to create a new Thread in Java. Firstly, you can extend the Thread class and override the run method to execute your code.

```
1  public class SayHello extends Thread {
2
3      public static void main(String[] args) {
4          new SayHello().start();
5      }
6
7      @Override
8      public void run() {
9          for (int i = 0; i < 100; i++) {
10             System.out.println("Hi there!");
11         }
12     }
13 }
```

Generally we avoid this. Java doesn't have multiple inheritance so this option will limit your ability to extend anything else. More importantly, it's just not a very pretty way of doing it. As good developers we aim to favour composition over inheritance. Option two is much nicer, allowing us to implement the Runnable interface and pass this to a new Thread object. The interface has one method on it, run.

```
1   public class SayHelloRunner implements Runnable {
2       public static void main(String[] args) {
3           new Thread(new SayHelloRunner()).start();
4       }
5
6       @Override
7       public void run() {
8           for (int i = 0; i < 100; i++) {
9               System.out.println("Hi there!");
10          }
11      }
12  }
```

We pass the new Runnable to a Thread to start it. We always use **start()** to run the thread; using run() will run execute in the same thread as the caller.

Q: How do we stop a Thread in java?

There is actually no API level way to stop a Thread reliably in java. The only guarantee is that when the code being executed in the thread completes, the thread will finish. It is therefore down to the developer to implement a way of telling a Thread to stop.

```
1   public class SayHelloRunner implements Runnable {
2       private volatile boolean running = true;
3
4       public void stopIt(){
5           running = false;
6       }
7
8       @Override
9       public void run() {
10          while(running)
11              System.out.println("Hi there!");
12      }
13  }
```

As you can see in the above example the flag to check if the thread is running or not has the keyword volatile.

Q:What is the volatile keyword?

In modern processors a lot goes on to try and optimise memory and throughput such as *caching*. This is where regularly accessed variables are kept in a small amount of memory close to a specific processor to increase processing speed; it reduces the amount the processor has to go to disk to get information (which can be very slow). However, in a multithreaded environment this can be very dangerous as it means that two threads could see a different version of a variable if it has been updated in cache and not written back to memory; *processor A* may think int i = 2 whereas *processor B* thinks int i = 4. This is where **volatile** comes in. It tells Java that this variable could be accessed by multiple threads and therefore should not be cached, thus guaranteeing the value is correct when accessing. It also stops the compiler from trying to optimise the code by reordering it.

The downside is that there is a performance penalty on using volatile variables. There is a greater distance to travel to get access to the information as it cannot be stored in the cache. However volatile is usually a much better option speed wise than using a synchronize block as it will not cause threads to block and as such is much faster than other options for synchronisation.

Q: Explain the synchronized keyword. What does it do? Why do we need it?

Synchronized is a keyword in java that can be used as a block around a piece of code or as part of the method signature.

```
1   public class Bank {
2       private int funds = 100;
3
4       public void deposit(int money){
5           synchronized (this){
6               funds += money;
7           }
8       }
9
10      public synchronized void withdraw(int money){
11          if(funds > money)
12              funds -= money;
13      }
14  }
```

Synchronized exists in Java to allow multiple threads which can both see an object to safely access it to ensure that the data is correct. The classic example is that of the bank account. Imagine if you remove the synchronisation from the above example. Thread one attempts to remove 100 from the account. At the exact same time, Thread two attempts to remove 100 from the account. For both threads when checking if there are sufficient funds the if statement returns true, resulting in them both withdrawing and a resultant balance of -100 which is not allowed. By using synchronized only a single thread can access the section of code in the synchronized block, which can help us to ensure correct state.

When a synchronized keyword is placed on a method such as on withdraw(int money), it has the same effect as wrapping all of a method's code in synchronized(this) (which is the case in the deposit method in the example). If any Thread tries to execute any synchronized method on the object it will be blocked.

Q: What are the downsides of using synchronized? How can we avoid or mitigate them?

Locks are slow. Really slow. Particularly when using the synchronized keyword, it can have a huge effect on performance. The reason for this is explained wonderfully in a paper LMAX created[3] on how they built Disruptor, a super low latency concurrency component. It is a brilliant read for anyone who wants to get into the fine details of threading and mechanical sympathy.

"Locks are incredibly expensive because they require arbitration when contended. This arbitration is achieved by a context switch to the operating system kernel which will suspend threads waiting on a lock until it is released. During such a context switch, as well as releasing control to the operating system which may decide to do other house-keeping tasks while it has control, execution context can lose previously cached data and instructions. This can have a serious performance impact on modern processors."

You don't need to learn the contents of the details of the quote; it should be sufficient to say that along with the impact of threads being blocked whilst they wait for a resource, there is an impact at an OS level which causes huge performance damage. In the same paper an experiment is carried out to see the impact on latency of different types of lock; without locking the process took 300ms, whereas with 2 threads contesting a lock it took 224,000ms. Getting threading right is hard but getting it wrong has huge consequences.

If you insist on using synchronized then minimising the size of the code block that is synchronized is a good start. The smaller this is will help to minimise impact. Even better, you can lock on specific objects, or use a lock object if using a primitive, so that the entire object does not need to be contended.

```
1   public class Bank {
2       private int funds = 100;
3       private Object fundLock;
4
5       private UserDetails details = new UserDetails();
6
7       public void deposit(int money){
8           synchronized (fundLock){ //Lock Object needs to be acquired to update fu\
9   nds
10              funds += money;
11          }
12      }
13
```

---

[3]http://lmax-exchange.github.io/disruptor/files/Disruptor-1.0.pdf

```
14      public void createUsername(){
15          synchronized (details){ //Lock on the details object mean that the detai\
16  ls object will block, but Bank will not.
17              details.setName("Bob");
18          }
19          System.out.println("His name is Bob");
20      }
21
22  }
```

Ideally though we want to avoid using synchronized where possible.

Q: What other options do we have for creating Thread safe code?

As previously discussed, making a variable volatile is more performant and less complex. However Java has a number of classes that aid us with threading so that we can do it in an efficient way.

The atomic classes

Q: What is CAS? What benefits does it have over Synchronized?

Java has a number of Atomic classes including AtomicInteger, AtomicDouble and AtomicBoolean. These are completely thread safe and do not involve locking, but instead use Compare and Swap (CAS) operations. A CAS operation is an atomic one (it happens as one single operation) where during an update we check that the field value has not changed from when we decided to update it (it hasn't been modified by another thread) and if so it sets the value to the new amount. This is exceptionally quick; CAS is actually an operation available on most processors and no blocking is required. It is still slower than single threaded (the LMAX experiment concluded it was 100x slower) but it is the best available away of ensuring thread safe access to values.

It is important to understand the difference between volatile and CAS. if you try and perform any operation that uses the original value it will render the volatile keyword useless. For example, $i++$ breaks down into $i = i + 1$. In the time between i being read (i + 1) and it being written (i = result) another thread can jump in between and update the value. Because the Atomic classes checks and writes values as an atomic operation, it is a much safer option.

Immutability

Immutable objects are brilliant. An immutable object is an object whose state cannot be changed after creation. By this definition all immutable objects are thread-safe. Programming to use immutable objects can be difficult and is a paradigm shift from standard object oriented programming. Functional languages like Scala make heavy use of immutable objects which allows them to scale well and be highly concurrent. The more we can rely on immutable objects the less threading we will need.

Thread methods

Q: What does yield() do?

The Thread class has a whole bunch of methods on it which you need to know for your interview. Interviewers love testing people on their ability to remember the details around these methods. It is best to read up on them before an interview.

Yield gives up the processor. Imagine you have a single CPU only. If a thread refuses to allow other threads CPU time they will remain permanently blocked. By calling yield() the thread is generously saying "who else wants a turn?". In reality it is unreliable and isn't normally used. The implementation can be different on any system or JVM, and can often be different between Java versions. There is no guarantee of what other thread will get the next access, nor when your thread will next get an opportunity to run.

Q: What does interrupt() do?

You may have noticed that a number of Thread related methods (most commonly Thread.sleep()) force you to catch an InterruptedException. If we need to suggest to a Thread it needs to stop for whatever reason we can do this by calling interrupt() on it. This sets the "interrupted" flag on the target thread. If the target thread chooses to check this flag (using the interrupted() or isInterrupted()) then it can optionally throw an Exception (usually Interrupted exception). It is predicated on the target Thread actually checking this. However there are a number of methods, such as Thread.sleep() which automatically poll for this flag. If the target thread is running one of these then an InterruptedException will be thrown straight away.

Q: What does join() do?

join() will simply tell the currently running thread to wait until completion of whichever thread join() is called on completes.

```
1   public class SayHelloRunner implements Runnable {
2
3       public static void main(String[] args) throws InterruptedException {
4           Thread thread = new Thread(new SayHelloRunner());
5           thread.start();
6           thread.join();
7           System.exit(3);
8       }
9
10      @Override
11      public void run() {
12          int i = 0;
13          while(i < 10000){
14              System.out.println(i);
15              i++;
```

```
16            }
17        }
18  }
```

In this example if we did not have the thread.join() the application will exit without printing anything out. The join() call effectively makes the call synchronous; it wants the Thread to finish before proceeding.

Object methods

Q: **What do wait(), notify() and notifyAll() do?**

wait(), notify() and notifyAll() are used as a means of inter-thread communication. When acquiring a lock on an object it may not be in the required state; perhaps a resource isn't set yet, a value isn't correct. We can use wait() to put the thread to sleep until something changes. When that something does change, the awaiting clients can be notified by calling notify() or notifyAll() on the object that is being waited for. If all of your waiting threads could in theory take action with the new information then use notifyAll(). However if there is a new lock to be acquired (so only one waiting Thread can take action), then call just notify().

Example:

```
1   public class Example {
2
3       public static void main(String[] args) {
4
5           ResourceCarrier carrier = new ResourceCarrier();
6           ThingNeedingResource thingNeedingResource
7           = new ThingNeedingResource(carrier);
8           ThingNeedingResource thingNeedingResource2
9           = new ThingNeedingResource(carrier);
10          ThingNeedingResource thingNeedingResource3
11          = new ThingNeedingResource(carrier);
12          ResourceCreator resourceCreator = new ResourceCreator(carrier);
13
14          new Thread(thingNeedingResource).start();
15          new Thread(thingNeedingResource2).start();
16          new Thread(thingNeedingResource3).start();
17          new Thread(resourceCreator).start();
18      }
19
20  }public class ResourceCarrier {
```

```
21      private boolean resourceReady;
22
23
24
25      public boolean isResourceReady() {
26          return resourceReady;
27      }
28
29      public void resourceIsReady() {
30          resourceReady = true;
31
32      }
33  }
34  public class ResourceCreator implements Runnable {
35      private ResourceCarrier carrier;
36
37      public ResourceCreator(ResourceCarrier carrier) {
38
39          this.carrier = carrier;
40      }
41
42      @Override
43      public void run() {
44          try {
45              Thread.sleep(2000);
46          } catch (InterruptedException e) {
47              e.printStackTrace();
48          }
49          synchronized (carrier) {
50              carrier.resourceIsReady();
51              carrier.notifyAll();
52          }
53      }
54  }
55  package com.core.interview.thread;
56
57
58  public class ThingNeedingResource implements Runnable {
59
60      private ResourceCarrier carrier;
61
62      public ThingNeedingResource(ResourceCarrier carrier){
```

```
63
64          this.carrier = carrier;
65      }
66      @Override
67      public void run() {
68          synchronized (carrier){
69              while(!carrier.isResourceReady()){
70                  try {
71                      System.out.println("Waiting for Resource");
72                      carrier.wait();
73                  } catch (InterruptedException e) {
74                      e.printStackTrace();
75                  }
76              }
77              System.out.println("haz resource");
78          }
79      }
80 }
81
82 Sample output:
83 Waiting for Resource
84 Waiting for Resource
85 Waiting for Resource
86 haz resource
87 haz resource
88 haz resource
```

In this example we have a wrapper around a resource called "Resource Carrier" and 3 threads that want access to its resource. When it acquires the lock it sees the resource isn't available and goes into wait mode by calling wait() on the ResourceCarrier object. The ResourceCreator swoops in later to create the resource and calls notify on the ResourceCarrier, at which point the three threads spring back to life.

Deadlock

Q: What is a deadlock?

Q: How do we prevent deadlocks?

Many candidates completely fluff the answer to deadlock questions. It's a very common interview question, and it's an easy enough concept to understand, but it can be tricky to explain (particularly over the phone).

A deadlock occurs when two or more threads are awaiting the actions of each other which prevents any further processing from happening. For example, Thread A has the lock on Object 1 and attempts to require a lock on Object 2 to continue. Simultaneously, Thread B has a lock on Object 2 and attempts to acquire a lock on Object 1. As a result both Threads are kept busy waiting for the other one, which will never release. This is a deadlock.

The easiest way to prevent deadlock is to ensure that the ordering of acquisition for locks is consistent. If both Threads try to acquire Object 1 then Object 2 in that order then deadlock will not occur. It is important to code defensively when acquiring locks. Even better is to make synchronized blocks as small as possible and where possible avoid locking multiple objects.

Q: What is Livelock?

In deadlock, the Threads will stop working and await the resource to become free. In Livelock the separate Threads do not stop; they will continue working trying to resolve the block. However, by doing so the blockage continues and will not resolve. This can happen in situations where, if a Thread cannot access the resources it requires it will go back to the start of processing and retry the work in a loop until success. Imagine the classic bank account example. If there is a simultaneous transaction from Account A to Account B and Account B to Account A then both accounts are debited, but when the crediting of the account takes place the account is already locked. The transactions are reverted and reattempted. This will continue ad infinitum with the work being attempted; hence, "live" lock.

Q: What is Thread Priority?

Thread has a method on it, setPriority() which takes an int representing the priority level. Thread has some constants on it you can use: Thread.MIN_PRIORITY, Thread.MAX_PRIORITY and Thread.NORM_PRIORITY.

However, like all things threading and JVM related, you cannot rely on it to behave in a consistent fashion particularly across different systems and operating systems. The actual way priority levels vary from system to system, and the CPU can choose to behave in any way it wants. Maybe for priorities above a certain level it will give a dedicated percentage of time. In the same fashion, you don't know what other processes are being run. You may have a background thread you set to a low value, but if there is some other process running on the machine at a slightly higher priority your Thread may never get run.

Nonetheless, it can work well. Check the following example:

```
1   public static void main(String[] args) {
2       Thread thread = new Thread(new Counter(1));
3       thread.setPriority(Thread.MAX_PRIORITY);
4       Thread threadTwo = new Thread(new Counter(2));
5       threadTwo.setPriority(Thread.MIN_PRIORITY);
6       thread.start();
7       threadTwo.start();
8   }
9
10  private static class Counter implements Runnable {
11      private int id;
12
13      public Counter(int i) {
14          id = i;
15      }
16
17      @Override
18      public void run() {
19          for (int i = 0; i < 10; i++) {
20              System.out.println("Thread " + id + " - " + i);
21          }
22      }
23  }
```

This simple program launches two Threads which count to ten in a loop. If I remove the priority setting lines, the output is jumbled:

```
1    Thread 2 - 0
2    Thread 1 - 0
3    Thread 1 - 1
4    Thread 1 - 2
5    Thread 1 - 3
6    Thread 1 - 4
7    Thread 2 - 1
8    Thread 2 - 2
9    Thread 2 - 3
10   Thread 2 - 4
11   Thread 2 - 5
12   Thread 2 - 6
13   Thread 1 - 5
14   Thread 1 - 6
15   Thread 2 - 7
```

```
16    Thread 2 - 8
17    Thread 1 - 7
18    Thread 1 - 8
19    Thread 1 - 9
20    Thread 2 - 9
```

However, if I run the program as it's shown above:

```
 1    Thread 1 - 0
 2    Thread 1 - 1
 3    Thread 1 - 2
 4    Thread 1 - 3
 5    Thread 1 - 4
 6    Thread 1 - 5
 7    Thread 1 - 6
 8    Thread 1 - 7
 9    Thread 1 - 8
10    Thread 1 - 9
11    Thread 2 - 0
12    Thread 2 - 1
13    Thread 2 - 2
14    Thread 2 - 3
15    Thread 2 - 4
16    Thread 2 - 5
17    Thread 2 - 6
18    Thread 2 - 7
19    Thread 2 - 8
20    Thread 2 - 9
```

Running on my machine this isn't consistent though, and does sometime jumble slightly. The way Threads work will never be consistent across machines or JVMs and it is important to write code that does not rely on a JVM's behaviour.

Q: What is Thread starvation?

If a Thread cannot get CPU time because of other Threads this is known as starvation. Imagine an extreme example like the above, with a number of high priority Threads and a single low priority Thread. The low priority is unlikely to get any CPU time and will be suffering from starvation.

Futures, callables and executors

Q: What is a ThreadPool? Why is it better to use them instead of manually creating Threads?

The creation and maintenance of Threads is expensive and time consuming. With a ThreadPool a group of Threads are available which can be called on to execute tasks. The Threads are created up-front, thus reducing the overhead at execution time. Once a task has been executed the Thread is returned to the pool to execute another task. If a Thread dies for some reason it will be replaced in the ThreadPool, removing the need to write complex Thread management code.

There is the added benefit that it makes it easy to control the number of tasks happening in parallel. For example, if we have a webserver we may want to limit the number of parallel tasks so that a huge burst of traffic wouldn't stop other background tasks from happening.

Q: How do you create a ThreadPool?

Normally ThreadPools are created using Executors.

```
1  ExecutorService executorService1 = Executors.newSingleThreadExecutor();
2  ExecutorService executorService2 = Executors.newFixedThreadPool(10);
3  ExecutorService executorService3 = Executors.newScheduledThreadPool(10);
```

A single thread executor will create a single thread; all tasks will be executed sequentially. The same could be achieved using Executors.newFixedThreadPool(1).

Executors.newFixedThreadPool will create a ThreadPool with exactly the number of Threads specified. Those threads will live for the lifetime of the JVM unless the Executor is shutdown using shutdown() (which will allow currently queued tasks to finish) and shutdownNow() (which will cancel any outstanding tasks).

Tasks can be run on ExecutorServices by either submitting a Callable or a Runnable.

Q: What is the difference between Callable and Runnable? What is a Future?

A Runnable cannot return a value and it cannot throw a checked exception, both features available in Callable. Often a return value is very useful when building multithreaded applications. When we submit a task to an executor we don't know when it will be executed; it could be instantly or at any time in the future- the whole process is asynchronous. Futures allow this to happen. Futures have one main method: get() and it's overloaded version, get(long timeout, TimeUnit unit). When called, it will block the current Thread whilst it awaits the result (if the result is not currently available).

There is no benefit/negative to using Callable over Runnable or vice versa; it all depends on whether a return value is needed.

```
1   public static void main(String[] args) throws InterruptedException, ExecutionExc\
2   eption {
3       Callable<String> callable = new StringCallable();
4       Callable<String> callable2 = new StringCallable();
5       Callable<String> callable3 = new StringCallable();
6       Callable<String> callable4 = new StringCallable();
7
8       ExecutorService executorService = Executors.newFixedThreadPool(4);
9       List<Future<String>> futures = executorService.invokeAll(asList(callable, ca\
10  llable2, callable3, callable4));
11      for (Future<String> future : futures) {
12          System.out.println(future.get());
13      }
14  }
15  //pool-1-thread-1
16  //pool-1-thread-2
17  //pool-1-thread-3
18  //pool-1-thread-4
```

Q: What is ThreadLocal?

ThreadLocal allows a different instance of a variable for each Thread that accesses it. Normally this will be a static variable used to store state like a UserID or session. This can also be particularly useful when an object is not Thread Safe but you want to avoid synchronising.

Big O Notation

I hate big O notation. For as long as I can remember it's been my biggest achilles heel. It's just something I've never managed to successfully motivate myself to learn about despite knowing it's going to come up in every single interview. I'll get asked to implement an algorithm which I'll do via brute force to start with: "What is the Big O of that?". "I don't know Big O but I know it's slow".

It's fairly obvious, but this is the wrong approach. Take the time to really read this chapter and maybe even do some extra research. This seems to be a question that comes up consistently at interviews so it's worth taking the time.

What on earth is Big O?

Big O is the way of measuring the efficiency of an algorithm and how well it scales based on the size of the dataset. Imagine you have a list of 10 objects, and you want to sort them in order. There's a whole bunch of algorithms you can use to make that happen, but not all algorithms are built equal. Some are quicker than others but more importantly the speed of an algorithm can vary depending on how many items it's dealing with. Big O is a way of measuring how an algorithm scales. Big O references how **complex** an algorithm is.

Big O is represented using something like O(n). The O simply denoted we're talking about big O and you can ignore it (at least for the purpose of the interview). *n* is the thing the complexity is in relation to; for programming interview questions this is almost always the size of a collection. The complexity will increase or decrease in accordance with the size of the data store.

Below is a list of the Big O complexities in order of how well they scale relative to the dataset.

O(1)/Constant Complexity: Constant. This means irrelevant of the size of the data set the algorithm will always take a constant time.

1 item takes 1 second, 10 items takes 1 second, 100 items takes 1 second.

It always takes the same amount of time.

O(log n)/Logarithmic Complexity: Not as good as constant, but still pretty good. The time taken increases with the size of the data set, but not proportionately so. This means the algorithm takes longer per item on smaller datasets relative to larger ones.

1 item takes 1 second, 10 items takes 2 seconds, 100 items takes 3 seconds.

If your dataset has 10 items, each item causes 0.2 seconds latency. If your dataset has 100, it only takes 0.03 seconds extra per item. This makes log n algorithms very scalable.

O(n)/Linear Complexity: The larger the data set, the time taken grows proportionately.

1 item takes 1 second, 10 items takes 10 seconds, 100 items takes 100 seconds.

O(n log n): A nice combination of the previous two. Normally there's 2 parts to the sort, the first loop is O(n), the second is O(log n), combining to form O(n log n).

1 item takes 2 seconds, 10 items takes 12 seconds, 100 items takes 103 seconds.

O(n^2)/Quadratic Complexity: Things are getting extra slow.

1 item takes 1 second, 10 items takes 100, 100 items takes 10000.

O(2^n): **Exponential Growth!** The algorithm takes twice as long for every new element added.

1 item takes 1 second, 10 items takes 1024 seconds, 100 items takes 1267650600228229401496703205376 seconds.

It is important to notice that the above is not ordered by the best to worst complexity. There is no "best" algorithm, as it completely hinges on the size of the dataset and the task at hand. It is also important to remember the code maintenance cost; a more complex algorithm may result in an incredibly quick sort, but if the code has become unmaintainable and difficult to debug is that the right thing to do? It depends on your requirements.

There is also a variation in complexity within the above complexities. Imagine an algorithm which loops through a list exactly two times. This would be O(2n) complexity, as it's going through your lists length (n) twice!

Why does this matter?

Simply put: *an algorithm that works on a small dataset is not guaranteed to work well on a large dataset.* Just because something is lightning fast on your machine doesn't mean that it's going to work when you scale up to a serious dataset. You need to understand exactly what your algorithm is doing, and what it's big O complexity is, in order to choose the right solution.

There are three things we care about with algorithms: **best case, worst case and expected case.** In reality we only actually care about the latter two, as we're a bunch of pessimists. If you ask an algorithm to sort a pre-sorted list it's probably going to do it much faster than a completely jumbled list. Instead we want to know the worst case (the absolutely maximum amount of steps the algorithm could take) and the expected case (the likely or average number of steps the algorithm could take). Just to add to the fun, these can and often are different.

Examples

Hopefully you're with me so far, but let's dive into some example algorithms for sorting and searching. The important thing is to be able to explain what complexity an algorithm is. Interviewers love to get candidates to design algorithms and then ask what the complexity of it is.

O(1)

Irrelevant of the size, it will always return at constant speed. The javadoc for Queue states that it is *"constant time for the retrieval methods (peek, element, and size)"*. It's pretty clear why this is the case. For peek, we are always returning the first element which we always have a reference to; it doesn't matter how many elements follow it. The size of the list is updated upon element addition/removal, and referencing this number is just one operation to access no matter what the size of the list is.

O(log n)

The classic example is a Binary search. You're a massive geek so you've obviously alphabetised your movie collection. To find your copy of "Back To The Future", you first go to the middle of the list. You discover the middle film is "Meet The Fockers", so you then head to the movie in between the start and this film. You discover this is "Children of Men". You repeat this again and you've found "Back to the Future". There's a great interactive demo of binary search available online at Armstrong State University[4].

Although adding more elements will increase the amount of time it takes to search, it doesn't do so proportionally. Therefore it is O(log n).

O(n)

As discussed in the collections chapter, LinkedLists are not so good (relatively speaking) when it comes to retrieval. It actually has a complexity of O(n) for the **worst case**: to find an element T, which is the last element in the list, it is necessary to navigate the entire list of n elements. As the number of elements increases so does the access time in proportion.

O(n log n)

The best example of O(n log n) is a **merge sort**. This is a divide and conquer algorithm. Imagine you have a list of integers. We divide the list in two again and again until we are left with with a number of lists with 1 item in: each of these lists is therefore sorted.We then merge each list with it's neighbour (comparing the first elements of each every time). We repeat this with the new composite list until we have our sorted result. To explain why this is O(n log n) is a bit more complex. In the above example of 8 numbers, we have 3 levels of sorting:

- 4 list sorts when the list sizes are 2
- 2 list sorts when the list sizes are 4
- 1 list sort when the list size is 8

[4]http://www.cs.armstrong.edu/liang/animation/web/BinarySearch.html

Now consider if I were to double the number of elements to 16: this would only require one more level of sorting. Hopefully you recognise this is a log n scale.

However, on each level of sorting a total of n operations takes place (look at the red boxes in the diagram above). This results in (n * log n) operations, e.g. O(n log n).

O(n^2)

The Bubble Sort algorithm is everyone's first algorithm in school, and interestingly it is quadratic complexity. If you need a reminder; we go through the list and compare each element with the one next to it, swapping the elements if they are out of order. At the end of the first iteration, we then start again from the beginning, with the caveat that we now know the last element is correct.

Imagine writing the code for this; it's two loops of n iterations.

```
1   public int[] sort(int[] toSort){
2       for (int i = 0; i < toSort.length -1; i++) {
3           boolean swapped = false;
4           for (int j = 0; j < toSort.length - 1 - i; j++) {
5               if(toSort[j] > toSort[j+1]){
6                   swapped = true;
7                   int swap = toSort[j+1];
8                   toSort[j + 1] = toSort[j];
9                   toSort[j] = swap;
10              }
11          }
12          if(!swapped)
13              break;
14      }
15      return toSort;
16  }
```

This is also a good example of best vs worst case. If the list to sort is already sorted, then it will only take one iteration (e.g. n) to sort. However, in the worst case we have to go through the list n times and each time looping another n items (less how many loops we have done before) which is slow.

You may notice that it's technically less than n^2 as the second loop decreases each time. This gets ignored because as the size of the data set increases this impact of this becomes more and more marginal and tends towards quadratic.

O(2^n)

Exponential growth! Any algorithm where adding another element dramatically increases the processing time. Take for example trying to find combinations; if I have a list of 150 people and

I would like to find every combination of groupings; everyone by themselves, all of the groups of 2 people, all of the groups of 3 people etc. Using a simple program which takes each person and loops through the combinations, if I add one extra person then it's going to increase the processing time exponentially. Every new element will double processing time.

In reality $O(2^n)$ algorithms are not scalable.

How to figure out Big O in an interview

This is not an exhaustive list of Big O. Much as you can $O(n^2)$, you can also have $O(n^3)$ (imagine bubble sort but with an extra loop). What the list on this page should allow you to do is have a stab in the dark at figuring out what the big O of an algorithm is. If someone is asking you this during an interview they probably want to see how you try and figure it out. Break down the loops and processing.

- Does it have to go through the entire list? There will be an *n* in there somewhere.
- Does the algorithm's processing time increase at a slower rate than the size of the data set? Then there's probably a *log n* in there.
- Are there multiple loops? You're probably looking at n^2 or n^3.
- Is access time constant irrelevant of the size of the dataset? *O(1)*

Sample question

I have an array of the numbers 1 to 100 in a random number. One of the numbers is missing. Write an algorithm to figure out what the number is and what position is missing.

There are many variations of this question all of which are very popular. To calculate the missing number we can add up all the numbers we do have, and subtract this from the expected answer of the sum of all numbers between 1 and 100. To do this we have to iterate the list once. Whilst doing this we can also note which spot has the gap.

```
1   public class BlankFinder{
2
3   public void findTheBlank(int[] theNumbers) {
4           int sumOfAllNumbers = 0;
5           int sumOfNumbersPresent = 0;
6           int blankSpace = 0;
7
8           for (int i = 0; i < theNumbers.length; i++) {
9               sumOfAllNumbers += i + 1;
10              sumOfNumbersPresent += theNumbers[i];
```

```
11          if (theNumbers[i] == 0)
12              blankSpace = i;
13          }
14
15          System.out.println("Missing number = " + (sumOfAllNumbers -
```

sumOfNumbersPresent) + " at location " + blankSpace +" of the array"); }

```
1    public static void main(String[] args) {
2        new BlankFinder().findTheBlank(new int[]{7,6,0,1,3,2,4});
3        }
4        //Missing number = 5 at location 2 of the array
5    }
```

Caveat: you can also calculate sumOfAllNumbers using (theNumbers.length+1) * (theNumbers.length) / 2.0). *I would never remember that in an interview though.*

What is the big O of your algo?

Our algorithm iterates through our list once, so it's **O(n)**.

Conclusion

You're amazing. Well done for reading this book all the way through. I'm very proud of it, but more specifically I'm proud of how I've been able to help people to get amazing new jobs. Whenever I get emails or messages through from people saying thanks because I've helped them to get a better job it gives me the biggest buzz.

If everything goes well and you've benefited from this, then please do let me know. Or even if you have extra questions, want someone to look over your CV, or just want to say hi. I try and reply to every message I get. I'm also available for one on one coaching and I'd love to help you, one on one, through your interview process. Drop me an email to discuss further.

e: hello@corejavainterviewquestions.com

t: @sambahk

Go out and ace that interview.

Sam

www.ingramcontent.com/pod-product-compliance
Lightning Source LLC
Chambersburg PA
CBHW041427050326
40689CB00003B/695